2/12/22

ETHICAL DILEMMAS IN QUALITATIVE RESEARCH

Cardiff Papers in Qualitative Research

About the Series

The Cardiff School of Social Sciences at Cardiff University is well known for the breadth and quality of its empirical research in various major areas of sociology and social policy. In particular, it enjoys an international reputation for research using qualitative methodology, including qualitative approaches to data collection and analysis.

This series publishes original sociological research that reflects the tradition of qualitative and ethnographic inquiry developed at Cardiff in recent years. The series includes monographs reporting on empirical research, collections of papers reporting on particular themes and other monographs or edited collections on methodological developments and issues.

Ethical Dilemmas in Qualitative Research

Edited by
TREVOR WELLAND
LESLEY PUGSLEY
Cardiff University, UK

ASHGATE

Published by
Ashgate Publishing Limited
Gower House
Croft Road
Aldershot
Hants GU11 3HR
England

Ashgate Publishing Company
131 Main Street
Burlington, VT 05401-5600 USA

Ashgate website: http://www.ashgate.com

British Library Cataloguing in Publication Data
Ethical dilemmas in qualitative research. - (Cardiff papers
   in qualitative research)
   1.Qualitative research - Moral and ethical aspects
   I.Welland, Trevor II.Pugsley, Lesley III.Cardiff
   University. School of Social and Administrative Studies
   300.7'2

Library of Congress Control Number: 2001099647

ISBN 0 7546 1350 X

Printed and bound by Athenaeum Press, Ltd.,
Gateshead, Tyne & Wear.

Contents

List of figures

Notes on contributors

Amanda Coffey is a Senior Lecturer in Sociology at the School of Social Sciences, Cardiff University. She has published on gender and education, qualitative research methods and analysis and on professional accountancy training.

Brian Davies is Professor of Education in the School of Social Sciences, Cardiff University. His research interests include the curricular and pedagogical aspects of schooling; educational policy; professional development; and social research.

Sara Delamont is Reader in the School of Social Sciences at Cardiff University. She has published widely on the sociology of education, the sociology and social history of women, qualitative research methods and European anthropology.

Bani Dev Makkar is a Research Officer at the London School of Economics. She was, until recently, a postgraduate student at the School of Social Sciences, Cardiff University.

Lesley Pugsley is a Lecturer in Research Methods at the School of Postgraduate Medical and Dental Education at UWCM. Her research interests include policy sociology into higher education markets and choice, gender issues and school transitions and she has published on these topics. She is currently researching the occupational socialisation of Pre-Registration House Officers in Wales and the South West of England.

Emma Renold is a Lecturer in the School of Social Sciences, Cardiff University, and, until recently, also a Research Assistant with the NSPCC where she is working on the violence programme looking at physical and sexual violence between young people in residential settings. Her PhD explores the construction of gender and sexual identities in the primary school.

Kate Robson is a Lecturer in Behavioural Science in the School of Dentistry at the University of Wales, College of Medicine. She has published work on the uses of computer mediated communications as a research tool and the role of the body in computerised communications.

Mark Robson is a Research Assistant at the School of Social Sciences, Cardiff University. His research interests include the effects of street theatre on space and the effects of the Internet on leisure.

Neil Selwyn is a Lecturer in the School of Social Sciences at Cardiff University. He has published widely on the educational use of Information Technology and is currently researching the development of the National Grid for learning (with John Fitz). His research interests include the construction of educational computing policy at the macro level of government and business, the development of educational information infrastructures and individual learners' psychological reactions to technology.

Catrin Smith is a Lecturer in Criminology at the Centre for Comparative Criminology and Criminal Justice at the University of Wales, Bangor.

Trevor Welland is a Lecturer in the School of Social Sciences, Cardiff University. His doctoral research explores the socialising consequences of training for ordained ministry within the Anglican Communion. Other teaching and research interests include teacher training, sociology of education and qualitative research methods.

Patrick White is a Research Fellow in the School of Social Sciences at Cardiff University. His doctoral research explores the Careers Education and Guidance offered to Year 11 pupils.

Emma Wincup is currently a Lecturer in Criminology and Criminal Justice at the University of Kent, Canterbury. Until recently she lectured in the School of Social Sciences, Cardiff University where she taught criminology and research methods to undergraduate and postgraduate students. Publications to date converge around two areas of interest: gender, crime and criminal justice (based on her doctoral research on bail hostel provision for women awaiting trial) and research methods in criminology. She has recently edited a volume in qualitative research in criminology in the Cardiff Papers Series. At present she is editing, and contributing to, a 'Handbook of Criminological Research' for Oxford University Press and an introductory text on crime for Hodder and Stoughton.

Introduction

LESLEY PUGSLEY AND TREVOR WELLAND

Qualitative research can cover a wide range of strategies of data collection, but central to the process is the reality of 'getting in and getting close to' the research participants. The characteristic connectedness and degree of intimacy that form between the researcher and the researched in qualitative research can generate a range of ethical issues. Concern about the ethical dimensions of social inquiry have prompted many of the professional associations (for example, the British Sociological Association, 1993) to publish their own sets of ethical guidelines which serve as critical reference points for novice and experienced researcher alike. In addition to these, the women's movement has served to develop a standpoint epistemology, which seeks to offer a non-exploitative relationship of collaboration and co-operation between the researcher and the researched.

Nevertheless, there are a number of elements that combine to inform the politics and the ethics of qualitative research, and there can be no definitive statements regarding the roles and relationships of the research process. There is a blurring of boundaries between the public and the private; the notion of 'informed' consents; acceptable levels of deception; and the possibilities of levels of 'harm' in all social study. The 'complexities and fluidity of the field' have led Punch (1994:84) to argue against a highly restrictive model of research. Rather he suggests qualitative researchers should simply 'do it', having first stopped to reflect on the political and ethical dimensions of their fieldwork. The broad aim of this book is to provide the reader with such an opportunity. It considers a range of issues relating to the ethical dimensions of the research process. The volume make use of narrative accounts to illustrate these debates, drawing on the reflections of the contributors as they define the dilemmas they encountered as they sought to navigate the uncharted territory of their respective fields.

The various chapters explore the inevitable tensions that arise in a diversity of settings and reinforce and serve as testament to the fact that prescriptive templates are unhelpful and, in many instances, untenable in providing an adequate foreshadowing of the perils and pitfalls encountered when researching the social. The book aims to explore and critically review some of the ethical features of qualitative research. These include, respect for privacy, establishing honesty and openness in the relationships formed, and guarding against the misrepresentation of the field setting or individuals within it.

Various inter-related issues emerge from the chapters. Firstly, the ethical dilemmas arising from particular roles or identities adopted by, or attributed to the researcher. The papers by Pugsley, White and Selwyn all derive from doctoral projects on educational issues concerned with choice of Higher Education Institution, Careers Education and Guidance, and the permeation of Information Technologies into classroom practice in sixth forms and FE colleges. Their papers focus on the ethical issues associated with various roles experienced whilst conducting in-depth interviews with the participants, or during the negotiation of access to research sites. They examine how participant expectations of the researcher, or outcomes of the research, can generate a number of unanticipated relational issues. The paper by Coffey will explore dimensions of sexual identity in fieldwork, and the ways in which desire and sex can be seen as aspects of the reality of the fieldwork experience.

Secondly, a number of the papers explore the range of issues arising from undertaking research in particular settings. Makkar concentrates on field relations and the ethical issues arising out of a research project conducted among poor women living at the periphery of Salvador, Brazil. Her chapter focuses upon the dilemmas that arise in the overseas context. Although some of them may be familiar territory, many are extenuated by the situation or made more blatant because of the geographical divides and ideological categories concerned. In contrast, Robson and Robson assess how traditional research ethics work in cyberspace, whilst Wincup and Smith focus on fieldwork in criminal justice settings.

Renold's chapter explores the ethical issues around rendering sexuality visible within the context of the primary school. As a relatively under-researched area, this chapter discusses what happens when private sexual experiences derived from talk about erections, condoms and wet dreams, are made public. Inner thoughts and feelings are reconstructed as disclosure of these experiences take place. Tensions that arise from being positioned as voyeur, confidante, colluder and sex therapist are explored alongside the more official public voices and imaginary moral panics of staff, parents and the media.

The chapter by Welland describes and elucidates the 'hybrid' nature of the realities involved in constructing an 'observer-as participant' role while researching the occupational preparation and socialisation of a group of full-time trainees for ordained ministry. It particularly focuses on the management of ethical issues and dilemmas arising from reciprocity and the inevitable interplay of truth, dissimulation and 'degrees of deceit' that emerged through an intense engagement with the social actors in this research setting. This chapter also explores the ways in which undertaking ethnographic field research for the first time resulted in confronting and deviating from anticipated 'idealistic' ethical principles derived from readings of professional codes of ethical conduct.

Two of the chapters explore the reflections of two well-established and highly respected qualitative researchers. The opening chapter by Davies draws on his rich experience as a researcher and, using action research as an example, he offers a critical and reflexive exploration of the relations of power, knowledge and ownership in the 'small change of research ethics'. Delamont revisits Becker's manifesto on values and methods and scrutinises his ideas and their utility for our era at the turn of the millennium.

This volume contributes to and extends the Cardiff Papers in Qualitative Research series. The various chapters contained in it serve to reflect some of the rich ethnographic and qualitative research that has been undertaken over recent years, in line with the long established Cardiff tradition. Many of the accounts draw on field experiences gained during the authors' doctoral research. As such they provide what may be seen as the 'private troubles' and reflections of the novice researchers as they become immersed and, at times, enmeshed in the various complexities and 'utter physicalities' of the research process. Other papers are from established researchers who draw on their extensive personal experiences to identify with the 'messy realities' of researching the social and, in so doing, demonstrate the need for reflection and responsibility in the research process.

References

BSA (British Sociological Association) (1993) *Statement of Ethical Practice*. Durham: BSA.

Punch, M. (1994) 'Politics and Ethics in Qualitative Research', in N.K. Denzin and Y.S. Lincoln (eds.) *Handbook of Qualitative Research*. London; Sage, 83 – 97.

1 Is action research good for you?

BRIAN DAVIES

We have long become accustomed to thinking of social theories as being or belonging to approach paradigms that have some of the characteristics of social or even religious movements (Gouldner, 1970; Bernstein, 1975). They are not only 'about' things but also 'for' and 'against' them. Models of society and human action employ language and ideas that are irremediably morally tinged. They speak necessity to believers and constitute danger, even an anathema, to those of alternative persuasion. Little wonder, then, that their procedures for self-renewal, their criteria and practices for evoking new knowledge, their 'methodologies', should provoke both pride and passion. Each has, at any given point of time and place, its guardians of more or less arcane practice whose last word is always final, until their next.

As with all specialised discourses, the inventions of those who produce new knowledge necessarily become recontextualised (Bernstein, 1996) and disseminated by lesser mortals, bearing the mutations of discipleship and use. How far the journey can be from wisdom to the intellectual wilderness is well exemplified by the often execrable debate about research paradigms in sociology and education. Since the timid landing of Chicagoan interactionism in the sixties (greeted by small indigenous bands of British Weberians and others of anthropological bent) provided respectable alternative to measurement and the survey, several generations of students have been treated to the crassest of versions of 'debate' over 'quantitative' and 'qualitative' methods, aka the 'virtues' of positivism and interpretivism. In it, methodological imputations of villainy and claims to saintliness have come as easily from the lips of street credibilitarians as from the daughters of ANOVA. Allegiance to 'positivism' has been claimed to give the blessing of objectivity, hypothesis testing and verification, careful

4

operationalisation of concepts, testing and measurement pictured as leading to even-handed versions of truth. Becoming interpretivist was, in contrast, to affirm the place of understanding others and their purposes, privileging meaning and the subjective, though very few have appeared to want to accept the logic of Blum's (1971) contention that the alternative to positivism is, indeed, poetry. Those in sociology who privilege meaning invariably claim to pursue understanding in objective ways. However, in the matter of whether or not they are 'positivists', if it does not count that they do not measure. In constructing their 'accounts' out of observation or interview material, they are typically merely substituting adjectival register for numbers.

There has never been any doubting the value-laden import of the positions taken on either side of the divide. The literature has abounded with death by a thousand cutting remarks visited by 'science' oriented methodologists upon the 'subjectivity', in effect, the wilful trading in ambiguity and even potential falsehood, of those who abjure the culture of conventional measurement procedures. In turn, puncturing the pretensions and uncovering the bad company kept by positivism assumed major forms of social and moral critique, for example, as in the world of the Frankfurt School from Horkheimer to Habermas (Frisby, 1974). American apostates, such as Cicourel (1964) and Garfinkel (1967) have provided critiques of measurement assumptions and the fragility of our understanding of the everyday base upon which the superstructures of grand theory are constructed that ought to bring smiles to the face even of those in the whitest of coats. And that the joke is permanent has become the postmodernist message inherited from the French lot who said that language always said what they meant, or vice versa.

As with social and religious movements, an increasingly respectable methodological position is the fence where, ever the toolmakers, eclectics enjoin the use of research methods in forms of paradigmatic pastiche where, usually, it is any attempt to operate experimentally that disappears fastest with the bathwater. On grounds very often presented as no stronger than an audit of pros and cons, the produce of different methods are seen to strengthen and ripen in the reflected glow of several paradigmatic suns. After all, after Marxist ethnography, anything was possible. And all the while, the mass of the 'research' population, under- and postgraduate students, drift into under-explicated eclecticism and/or relativism. It is not so much that methodological polytheism is wrong - the gods were made in our image to serve us - but that it tends to make us too satisfied too easily with mere juxtaposition. Triangulation may sometimes be beside the point and play, end in itself though it is, it does not necessarily do the work of analysis.

To all of this, I want to put Oakley's (1999:252) question 'what are research methods *for*?', expecting an answer, even in our era of multiple meanings, that 'the aim of research methods is to provide some sort of approximation to what is 'really going on' expressing concern 'about the extent to which different research methods offer protection against bias, the possibility that we will end up with misleading answers', meeting the requirement that '*all* methods must be open, consistently applied and replicable by others'. Oakley's trajectory from a developed reputation for, to a worried frown about, 'qualitative' research would, in terms of this criterion, find echo with many of us. In my own attempts to 'do research' over the past forty years, means and morals have always appeared elaborately intertwined. 'Methods' seemed to be as much answers to the problems of keeping researchers and their objects/subjects/collaborators/ victims apart or 'square' as they were designed to bring them together. Research as truth made public (yes, even 'whose truth?' and 'what truth?') carried licence to expose, granted by? My own origin among the only too well aware proletariat imbued me with a deep and, I think, healthy distrust of those carrying warrants to interrogate. I remain the world's stroppiest research respondent, insatiably curious as to the ends to which my words may be put. Those same origins, as with work itself, even when carrying the privileges of academia, have inclined me always to disbelief that anyone should actually like either. An it has long struck me that the small change of research ethics - asking people nicely, not getting in the way, promising no names, keeping secrets, not interfering - buys only the sweeties and light snacks in what *can* be a devouring relation of power, knowledge and ownership that critical theorists pointed to and Foucault (1970) inscribed on recent social science consciousness.

The issue, as ever, is living with the paradox. Things can be both good and bad for you. Just as the profit motive is touched by irremediable immorality (just as Mam and Marx always insisted), so in the terms of one of my earliest doctoral students (jointly supervised with Mark Blaug), it was also evident that 'modern capitalism is in general terms a brilliant civilisation, based on the *individual* decision maker', having 'extraordinary power of socialisation', establishing 'deep internalised frames on the citizenry, as the condition of the dissolution of external, often coercive frames' (O'Keeffe, 1980:83). Just as market and class codes coexist in (post) capitalist society so, in the same sort of way, the old story about who knows better or best has always seemed to me to be partly a matter of context and voice - no-one knows me better or worse than myself, though many different others may say truly of me what I neither assent to or know (or may even be capable of knowing) - and of ideology, defining me not in my own but others' interests. The sixties, seventies and eighties had no shortage of those who 'knew best', crazy egalitarians, common sense freaks and weak professionals, while the nineties has revealed how easily our dominant new middle classes sign up to the advantages of the inegalitarianism of the performative educational state.

It was my earliest encounters as a teacher with school organisational and classrooms that impelled me toward seeking mainly sociological answers to such puzzles. Why were schools and schooling dominated by ideas and practices that enshrined hierarchic pupil ability? Why did teachers, even when they knew a great deal about subject matter, know so little and share even less about why and how they taught? While, for me, these questions altered their focus and emphases over the years, not least under the influence of Basil Bernstein. It always seemed to be the case that teachers' missing mystery, what I initially saw as their weak technology that gave them, as characteristically put-upon practitioners, little scope, in Crozier's (1972) terms, for solving crises, let alone causing them in the first place, was what Bernstein called pedagogy's 'missing voice'. Its processes, pedagogic discourse, seemed destined to act only as a relay for others (Bernstein, 1995). Teachers researching their own or local practices, almost certainly weakly socialised into discourses outside of their subject or stage-truncated versions of psychological developmentalism seemed, more than most, to require sight of a world of discourse outside of their own in order to go round other than in circles.

It is for these sorts of reasons that I contend that the past thirty years has seen an equally serious assault on methodological standards and meanings from those devoted to a variety of 'action research' approaches. Much of it that one sees at the level of student projects and dissertations at undergraduate or Masters' level is merely ignocent, a mixture of ignorance and innocence licensed by higher education teachers and texts against whom our anger ought to be directed. What the student is encouraged or even required to do is to examine 'own practice'. The activity of describing some limited state of affairs, very often in their own classroom, or among a group of colleagues, or at the institutional level, is regarded as its own justification: it is 'action research' and may lucky-dip into the method box in assembling information. Its end is declared to be 'improvement', though the enormities of establishing criteria and evidence for this, outside of personal perception of one's own performance, are usually neither adduced nor dealt with. Nearer the frontier of this research production mode, things are not necessarily much better. Most versions refer to a cyclical process of searching for improvement in personal or collective practice. Sometimes, the individual is enjoined to record experience and reflection. At others, a group involvement is regarded as essential and a quasi-therapeutic, truth-telling engagement encouraged. In most versions there is a celebration of the need for open and co-operative collegial relations in achieving improvement or change, although commitment to them, as in Wallace (1986), is no guarantee of their achievement. Records and measures of progress, particularly as available from students' work and opinions, are regarded as relevant evidence. But the question is 'of what? What is educational action research a case of?'

In his brief review of education and research, 1960-75 Nisbet (2000) argues that the unprecedented expansion of funding in the 1960s (albeit from subventing two men and a dog to a small herd of young bulls, the odd maverick and a flock of sheep) rapidly gave way to government control and attacks on its autonomy. In an essentially technocratic climate '(N)ew styles of research (such as action research and case study) challenged traditional patterns of experimental design and statistical analysis' (p.410). Though Nisbet says nothing more about the purchase of these 'new styles on British action research', there is a well established view that they were tied together as a 'movement' originating in the problems encountered by Stenhouse in framing and running the Schools' Council Humanities Curriculum Project from 1967 and those with whom he collaborated and influenced, including Elliott, McDonald, Walker, Adelman and Ruddock. In the main, then, it grew out of particular attempts to modify and accommodate traditional notions of standards and culture to the uncharted territory of curricular forms and teaching practices that might make mass secondary education less divisive and more inclusive.

The 'teacher as researcher' (Stenhouse, 1975) was born out of the ruckus engendered over the HCP's employment of them as 'neutral chairmen'. Having hit the rocks of established educational discourse, as ever capable only of speaking with the voice of dominant others, means were sought to avoid future, unwinnable confrontation, to make progress.   A spate of publications, initially arising from the Ford Teaching Project, characterised the mid-seventies (e.g. Elliott, 1976; Elliot and Adelman, 1976; McDonald, 1976; Walker and Adelman, 1977). The construction of the Eat Anglican redoubt has continued ever since, careful of its alliances, drawn toward networking, keen on publicisation, not least because of the tenuousness of its connections with conventional bases of research power and privilege though, indicatively, well placed in the British Educational Research Association.

Action research is now not one but several things, with a substantial mainstream commentative literature in Britain, ranging from the hagiographic to post-modern playful and including funded research work on the life histories of a selection of its own main protagonists (e.g. Nixon, 1981; McNiff, 1988; Hustler, Cassidy and Cuff, 1986; Elliott and Sarland, 1995; Stonach and Maclure, 1997; and Winter, 1989). There is a wider 'researching teaching' literature, some of which privileges 'action research' and 'reflective practice', as represented by Loughran's (1999) collection, in which van Manen (1999:26) notes that, *qua* Freire, Apple and Giroux, for 'many North Americans, pedagogy automatically means critical pedagogy, and its agenda is more dedication to social change than to the educational lives of young people'. A distinctive US variation is represented in the Burnaford, Fischer and Hobson (1996:xi) volume 'intended for classroom and apprentice teachers who are interested in knowing more about ways to participate with students in classroom research'. An equally characteristic British variation in terms of 'problem-based action research ... derived from the philosophy of Karl Popper' is outlined by Swann and Ecclestone (1999:92). In the same volume, research hunter-general, Tooley (1999:176), OFSTED licensed, Woodhead inspired rejecter of all relativisms, reassures us that, in terms of evolutionary epistemology, such as that of Ruse (1996), 'scientific method ... is built into our genes, and this is why it works and is shared by all humanity' (p.176). Our most accomplished tool users in educational research, the US managers, administrators and improvers have been known to regard action research as 'the process of systematically evaluating the consequences of educational decisions and adjusting practice to maximise effectiveness' (McLean, 1995:3) while. Britain's Crawford, Kydd and Parker (1994) *Educational Management in Action* contains nothing, in this respect, more practitioner oriented than SWOT analysis in the twenty case study investigations reported. Finally, Middlewood, Coleman and Lumby (1999:19) endorse action research *qua* Elliott (1991) and Schön (1984), despite noting 'a number of potential paradoxes in practitioner research', quoting, without approving, Cochran-Smith and Lytle (1998:31) in believing that the latter amounts to 'a new paradigm that aims to frontally transform rather than describe a school or classroom setting'.

Amidst these complications and voices, the target that I wish to address is the fate of perfectly ordinary teacher folk who seek more or less guided choices on how to deepen their understanding of their work and educational issues, more generally, by investigative activity. I take it for granted that to understand better is to increase the relevant basis upon which to make or recommend choice for practice. Such teachers have become the objects of desire not only of higher education but Government and their own professional associations. Following twenty years of denigration of educational research of all sorts, under a succession of Tory and New Labour Governments, Secretary of State for Education Blunkett has offered conditional rapprochement (Hammersley, 2000) to the research community. Among other new forms of support, up to £3 million in 'Best Practice Research Scholarships' was promised to teachers during the school year 2000-2001, through the Standards Fund. Individual teachers might expect to receive up to £3,000, while applications may also be made via supporting organisations for collective activity. Proposals in areas central to current policy are 'particularly welcome' (DfEE, 2000:11) for 'classroom based and sharply focussed small scale studies in priority areas, and to apply and disseminate their findings'. Both the NUT and NASUWT are now also offering the same sorts of individual sums, while the ATL claims to use member research to inform its policy documents. They see such help as part of members' career and professional development as well as being part of a service to make research findings more accessible to them (Kirkman, 2000). It is not yet at all clear how much of this research has been funded within a distinctive action research framework.

What, indeed, is now truly distinctive about such a framework in the British context? The outsider's empirical gambit in searching for an answer would be to find the home journal, in this case *Educational Action Research,* now in eight volumes, whose editors (Day, Elliott, Somekh, Winter, Green), associate editors (mainly overseas, including names from Scotland and Ireland but not Wales) and editorial panel (including Carr and Whitehead) stand for a broad and inclusive AR church. Carr (1999:173), the movement's most widely cited theorist, is quite clear that Elliott, direct heir and refiner to Stenhouse 'has become the principal architect and chief exponent of a distinctive tradition of educational enquiry' serving research, policy analysis and theoretical critique. 'Critical educational enquiry', in Carr's (1995:77) terms, arises out of the 'question of whether scientific standards have any place in educational research at all'. Far from simply connoting a preference for interpretative approaches to educational research, it involves questioning the adequacy of all conventional research activities. Human activities make sense only in terms of purpose and education is 'a practical activity the purpose of which is to change those being educated in some desirable ways'. Its problems are solved by doing, so that 'educational research that simply transforms educational problems into a series of theoretical problems seriously distorts the purpose of the whole enterprise' (p.79). Outside researchers simply have no place in tackling problems that exist within practitioners' theoretical frameworks. Educational theory

> is not something 'derived from' or 'based on' the theories *about* education that are produced by the theoretical social sciences ... it refers to a conceptual framework that expresses how those engaged in some particular activity ought to proceed.

Closing gaps in educational theory and practice refers to 'improving the theories employed by practitioners to make sense of their practices' (p.81). Naturalist social science approaches that overlook the theoretical power of educational practitioners are not really concerned with educational problems. In contrast, even though interpretative approaches may root themselves in explicating practitioner frameworks, these must be not only related to their practices and their adequacy but point to alternative, better ones. Carr's preferred direction for the resolution of these issues is that 'educational science' shall investigate activity 'which can only be identified and understood by reference to the meaning it has for those who practice' and 'tries to develop theories that explain and resolve the problems to which the practice of this activity gives rise' (p.83). It should be characterised by an historically aware fallibilism, as science itself now is, whose

> problem-solving judgements ... are governed by norms and principles designed to explore and eliminate the inadequacies in existing theoretical understanding and, hence, to encourage progressive, theoretical development and change;

of which the 'unquestioning "common sense" attitude' of education stands in need (p.85). Educational practice becomes the test bed for theory and its practitioners active participants.

Whitehead (1993) is for dialogue and unhappy with reliance on propositional forms of knowledge, to which he sees even reflective practitioner theorists, like Schon, being limited. He wants to direct our attention 'to the living individuals and contexts within which a living theory is being produced' in answer to the question 'How do I improve my practice?' (Whitehead, 1993:69). Its pursuit entails adoption of an action reflection cycle by an 'I' as 'a living contradiction' (p.70) which moves from recognition of values being negated in practice, imagining solutions, acting on them, evaluating outcomes and modifying the problem, etcetera. In this process, he sees himself going beyond Carr, Elliott, Hirst, Habermas and Gadamer in arguing that those who pursue the value laden practices of education must, individually and co-operatively, be committed to a process of social validation among participants who 'suppose that the validity claims they reciprocally raise are justified'. In sharing assumptions they may achieve 'theory with some potential for generalisibility' (p.73), whose focus is the relationship between practitioners' accounts and their practice. In the politics of truth, we must speak for ourselves.

Among professional action researchers, Whitehead's type of position, is probably about the limit point of rejection of conventional notions of research authority and governance, echoed in the reliance on the mutually validated record of feelings and practice associated with work inspired at Denbigh School, though such an artefact has a somewhat attenuated relation with what the historical Stenhouse intended for the use of case record.

What might stand, most obviously, as the mainstream characterisation of action research before the 1988 deluge, as represented, for example, by Hustler et al. (1986) was the case study in which teachers, at the very least badly served by conventional investigators, conduct classroom enquiry in schools using tape and notes as their means of making a record. They both research and act in ways which respect or incorporate children's perspectives, seeking 'intellectual space' either to generalise action themselves or, with outside research help, the means to move beyond 'safe' into more challenging change. Winter's (1989) picture, conceived as the clouds gathered, is perhaps the most connected and clearest account of the issues at stake. He was anxious to provide for practices accessible to all, rather than all-encompassing exercises suited only to the saintly and workaholic teacher. Taking it for granted that methods, *per se*, were not the issue but, rather, that access to them (no previous experience or 'ology' necessary) and the uses to which they were put, constituted the problem, Winter elaborated six principles involving reflexive and dialectical critique: collaborative resource; risk; plural structure; and linking theory, practice and transformation.

I have no doubt that his emphases on finding ways in which individuals will risk change and upon the importance of plurality in reporting and critique are of great strength. But his insistence upon the beastliness of 'positivism', evident at more or less depth and cogency across all action research specifications, rests on depicting it as relying on method. But hard or, as here, bad cases never make for good law or even a decent nostrum. The world is full of cases of 'bad' positivism, of both the quantitative and qualitative kind, that rely on the rituals of method as form rather than 'languages of description' (Bernstein, 1996) as translation devices of any adequacy. It is the absence or inadequacy in such studies of appropriate linkage of their theoretical or conceptual terms, of our specialised languages and their empirical referents, that make them 'bad'. In the social sciences and education, the tendency toward horizontal knowledge structures with weak grammars produces languages 'based on different, usually opposing, epistemological/ideological/social assumptions' so that

> the relation between them cannot be settled by empirical research. The relations can only be those of critique. Each specialised language, or rather, their sponsor and authors, may accuse the others of failures of omission and/or epistemological/ideological/social inadequacies of the assumptions (Bernstein, 1999:171).

Just as good ethnographers will know that 'learning the language' may be prerequisite to entering members' lives, so they will also accept that 'cultures are not transparent' and knowing the rules for contextual use may merely 'enable members to work the culture but not to know its workings'. Moving beyond being

> marooned in ... specific contexts and their enactments' requires the creation of an external language of description which must be derived from the internal language but 'capable of going beyond the description created by members.

While it provides the realisation and recognition rules for identifying 'the manifest contingent enactments of ... empirical relations' it must, for pragmatic and ethical reasons, remain free of the internal so as to allow for change in the latter and the opportunity for the researcher to 're-describe the descriptions made of them' while also remaining 'permeable to the potential enactments of those being described' (Bernstein, 1996:137-8).

If Winter's tale, or that of any action researcher, is to pass as being about 'research', and this is no semantic quibble, the issue facing it is the same as that facing ethnography or any of the specialised sociological or educational research languages. In Bernstein's (1999:170) terms, can we shift our 'gaze', where we privilege how we

> recognise, realise and cultivate legitimately the phenomena of concern ... from commitment to a language to dedication to a problem and its vicissitudes ... from the specialised languages to issues of empirical description?

I have long argued that teachers provide, if not the last, then the best home for altruism, as large workforces go. Their ability to mind the shop fairly, as producers under non-market criteria looks increasingly good in retrospect from our benchmarked present. Until we have stronger warrant for its changed intentions, a government that stops hating 'research', especially the bits fixed by its bespoke suppliers, and starts subventing teachers to carry it out, must be regarded as merely furthering by other means its recently discovered prowess of having both first and last words. 'Evidence-based practice is a backlash to, or an advance on, what? The crucial issues are not only 'whose evidence?' but also 'what evidence?' Just as it has been wrong and bullying for governments to requisition detailed educational control by a process of first rubbishing teacher effort and belief, so they have displayed great shallowness of understanding in modelling change on the belief that 'raising standards' or 'improvement' is a matter of 'copying the best'.

Atkinson (2000) puts a number of these issues succinctly. The milestones on the road to really useful official knowledge provided by Hargreaves, Hillage, Reynolds and Tooley ought to be seen not as '*end product*' or destinations but each as the "*beginning*" of an essential process of discourse and debate' (p.322), the purpose of educational research being

> not merely to provide 'answers' to the problems of the next decade or so, but to continue to inform discussion, among practitioners, researchers and policy-makers and researchers, about the nature, purpose and content of the educational enterprise (p.328).

Neither brutish rejections of theory, mechanistic views of its link with practice, pick 'n mix partisanship, nor models of 'relatively controlled relationship between practitioners, policy-makers and researchers' (p.321) are appropriate to the public intellectual role of the researcher in a democracy. She rightly insists that teacher heads (or knowledge bases) are full of 'theory', many voices from social science, philosophy and their everyday experience. The real battle is not about 'no theory' or abandoning method but about whose shall be privileged.

In such a context of policy and control, the inescapable linkages of power and research, the issues of who is originating, who is implementing, who is listening, who are issuing the warrants to enter and act in research that is increasingly 'for the State', pose acute questions. Although addressing better understanding of practice, action research projects have always seemed to me, along with a variety of other standpoint epistemologies, to be unstable, to rely on undemonstrated claims to interior authenticity. Substituting good faith or feeling good for good public evidence, demonstrably well theorised, is no solution. It would be essentially absurd if, in seeking freedom from imposition, action research became merely chained to the local. Its leading edge protagonists will immediately eschew this as intention or effect. But they are not its only or main practitioners. Those are the numerous students and teachers seeking professional renewal who receive it as a recontextualised discourse where a confessional narrative becomes the means of absolution for care and depth in thinking beyond the local in their topic, its means of investigation or how to count the rows of beans that it may generate. We already have a generation of teachers in our schools for most of whom the events of the 1988 Act and after constitute their entire horizon. To what questions are their increasingly guided questions answers?

References

Apple, M. (1990) *Ideology and the Curriculum*, 2nd Edition, New York, Routledge and Kegan Paul.

Atkinson, E. (2000) In Defence of Ideas, or Why 'What Works' is Not Enough. *British Journal of Sociology of Education*, 21, 3, 317-330.

Bernstein, B. (1975) The sociology of education: a brief account, in *Class, codes and control*, Vol. 3, Towards a Theory of Educational Transmission, London, Routledge and Kegan Paul.

Bernstein, B. (1996) *Pedagogy, Symbolic Control and Identity*, London, Taylor and Francis.

Bernstein, B. (1999) Vertical and Horizontal Discourse: an essay. *British Journal of Sociology of Education*, 20, 2, 157-173.

Blum, A.F. Theorising, in J.D. Douglas (Ed.) *Understanding Everyday Life*, London, Routledge and Kegan Paul.

Burnaford, G., Fischer, J. and Hobson, D. (Eds.) (1996) *Teachers Doing Research - Practical Possibilities*? Mahwal, New Jersey, Lawrence Erlbaum.

Carr, W. (1995) *For Education: Towards Critical Educational Enquiry*, Buckingham, Open University Press.

Carr, W. (1999) Book review: The Curriculum Experiment: meeting the challenge of social change by John Elliott, 1998 in *Educational Action Research*, 7, 1, 173-176.

Carr, W. and Kemmis, S. (1986) *Becoming Critical: Education, Knowledge and Action Research*, London, Falmer Press.

Cicourel, A.V. (1964) *Method and Measurement in Sociology*, New York, MacMillan.

Cochran-Smith, M. and Lytle, S.L. (1998) Teacher research: The question that persists. *International Journal of Leadership in Education: Theory and Practice*, 1, 1, 19-36.

Crawford, M., Kydd, L. and Parker, S. (Eds.) (1994) Educational Management in Action. A collection of case studies, London, Paul Chapman and The Open University.

Crozier, M. (1972) *The Bureaucratic Phenomenon*, London, Tavistock.

DfEE (2000) *Best Practice Research Scholarships. Guidance Notes for Teacher Applications*, Nottingham, DfEE Publications.

Dixon, J. (1981) *A Teacher's Guide to Action Research*, London, Grant McIntyre.

Elliott, J. and Adelman, C. (1976) *Innovation at the Classroom Level: A Case Study of the Ford Teaching Project, CE 203*, Milton Keynes, Open University Press.

Elliott, J. (1976) *Developing Hypotheses about Classrooms from Teacher Practical Constructs*, Cambridge, Cambridge Institute of Education.

Elliott, J. (1991) *Action Research for Educational Change*, Milton Keynes, Open University Press.

Elliott, J. and Sarland, C. (1995) A study of 'teachers as researchers' in the context of award-bearing courses and research degrees, *British Educational Research Journal*, 21, 3, 371-386.

Foucault, M. (1970) *The Order of Things: An Archaeology of the Human Sciences*, London, Tavistock.

Freire, P. (1970) *Pedagogy of the Oppressed*, New York, Seabury Press.

Frisby, D. (1974) The Frankfurt School: critical theory and positivism in J. Rex (Ed.) *Approaches to Sociology. An introduction to major trends in British sociology*, London, Routledge and Kegan Paul.

Garfinkel, H. (1967) *Studies in Ethnomethodology*, Englewood Cliffs, New Jersey, Prentice-Hall.

Giroux, A. M. (1981) Pedagogy, pessimism and the politics of conformity. A reply to Linda McNeil, *Curriculum Enquiry*, 11, 3, 211-222.

Gouldner, A.W. (1970) *The coming crisis of Western Sociology*, New York, Basic Books.

Hammersley, M. (2000) The Sky Is Never Blue For Modernisers: The Threat Posed by David Blunkett's Offer of 'Partnership' to Social Science, *Research Intelligence*, 72, June, 12-13.

Hargreaves, D.H. (1996) *Teaching as a Research-Based Profession: possibilities and prospects.* Teacher Training Agency Annual Lecture 1996, London, Teacher Training Agency.

Hustler, D., Cassidy, T. and Cuff, T. (Eds.) (1986) *Action Research in Classrooms and Schools*, London, Allen and Unwin.

Kirkman, S. (2000) Doing it for themselves, *Times Educational Supplement*, April 14, p.22.

Loughran, J. (Ed) (1999) *Researching Teaching. Methodologies and Practice for Understanding Pedagogy*, London, Falmer.

McDonald, B. (1976) Evaluation and the control of education in D. Tawney (ed.) *Curriculum Evaluation Today*, London, McMillan,

McLean, J.E. (1995) *Improving Education Through Action Research. A Guide for Administrators and Teachers*, Thousand Oaks, California, Corwin Press.

McNiff, J. (1988) *Action Research: principles and practice*, London, MacMillan Education.

Middlewood, D., Coleman, M. and Lumby, J. (Eds.) (1999) *Practitioner Research in Education: Making a Difference*, London, Paul Chapman.

Nisbet, J. (2000) When the 'Rot' Set In: education and research, 1900-75, *British Educational Research Journal*, 26, 3, 409-421.

Oakley, A. (1999) Paradigm wars: some thoughts on a personal and public trajectory. *International Journal of Social Research Methodology*, 2, 3, 247-254.

O'Keeffe, D.J. (1980) *The Sociology of Human Capital*, Unpublished PhD, Institute of Education, University of London.

Popper, K.R. (1979) *Objective knowledge: An Evolutionary Approach*, Oxford, Oxford University Press.

Reynolds, D. (1998) *Teacher Effectiveness: better teachers, better schools*, Teacher Training Agency Annual Lecture 1998, London, Teacher Training Agency.

Ruse, M. (1986) *Taking Darwin Seriously: A Naturalistic Approach to Philosophy*, Oxford, Basil Blackwell.

Schön, D.A. (1984) Leadership as reflection-in-action, in T. Sergiovanni and J. Corbally (Eds.) *Leadership and Organizational Culture*, Urbana and Chicago, University of Illinois Press.

Stenhouse, L. (1975) *An Introduction to Curriculum Research and Development*, London, Heinemann.

Stronach, I. and McLure, M. (1997) *Educational Research Undone*, Buckingham, Open University Press.

Swann, J. and Ecclestone, K. (1999) Empowering Lecturers to Improve Assessment Practice in Higher Education in J. Swann and J. Pratt (Eds.) *Improving Education. Realist Approaches to Method and Research*, London, Cassell.

Tooley, J. (1998) *Educational Research: a review*, London, Office for Standards in Education/HMSO.

Tooley, J. (1999) The Popperian Approach to Raising Standards in Educational Research in J. Swann and J. Pratt (Eds.) *Improving Education. Realist Approaches to Method and Research*, London, Cassell.

Van Manen, M. (1999) The language of Pedagogy and the Primacy of Student Experience, in J. Loughran (Ed) (1999) *Researching Teaching. Methodologies and Practice for Understanding Pedagogy*, London, Falmer.

Walker, R. and Adelman, C. (1975) *A Guide to Classroom Observation*, London, Methuen.

Wallace, A.M. (1986) *Towards an Action Research Approach to Educational Management*, Unpublished PhD, University of East Anglia.

Whitehead, J. (1993) *The Growth of Educational Knowledge. Creating Your Own Living Educational Knowledge, Bournemouth*, Hyde Publications.

Winter, R. (1980) Learning *from Experience. Principles and Practice in Action Research*, Lewes, The Falmer Press.

2 Putting your oar in: moulding, muddling or meddling?

LESLEY PUGSLEY

Introduction

Kids may tell them a lot or a little. If a lot, it is of course filtered by what kids think is fit for their parents' ears. If a little, parents have only infrequent contacts with teachers, casual discussions with other parents, and school reports to fill out the picture.

While it can be argued that all social study is intrusive and invasive, it is frequently undertaken to explore, and make sense of, 'filtration processes' such as those identified by Connell, et al. (1982:54). In order to arrive at such an understanding, as Hammersley and Atkinson (1995) note, the researcher spends time observing and recording and possibly, on occasions, even participating in some aspects of the subjects' lives, their daily routines and experiences. This chapter draws on one such ethnographic study focused on sixth form pupils as they and their families were engaged [or not] with the market in higher education and issues of choice (Pugsley, 1998). It considers the external time constraints imposed on the researcher, and the concomitant ethical dilemmas such pressures may realise in respect of 'informed consents' and reciprocity in field relations. It highlights the tensions, which are exacted, and the impact on decisions taken in the field, some of which sit uncomfortably within the paradigm of feminist researcher.

Researching in educational settings raises particular ethical issues (Ball, 1981; Burgess, 1983) and this chapter sets out to explore [some of] these. It illustrates how, in the process of obtaining data which provide rich descriptive accounts, the very strengths of a qualitative study, the researcher is required to take decisions, the consequences of which may well remain as a source of reflection and 'if only....' long after the field work is completed.

The research setting

Fieldwork was conducted in ten schools in south east Wales, and sought to address the decision making processes associated with young people and their families engaged in higher education choices. The data collection methods included questionnaires, focus groups and semi-structured interviews with the sixth form pupils at key stages of the choice process. Ethnographic interviews were conducted with key members of staff in each school and home based, in depth, semi-structured interviews with pupils and their families. The school sites were drawn from a purposive sample in order to ensure a breadth of 'type'. The fieldwork began at the start of the academic year, when the pupil cohort had just entered the first of their two years of sixth form education.

In total some 760 pupils participated in the overall study, of which 60 took part in focus group interviews and 20 in semi-structured interviews with their families. The project is located within a theoretical framework of social and cultural reproduction in higher education (Bourdieu and Passeron, 1990). This perspective is used in order to discuss the hierarchies of choice in relation to class based sponsorship. The focus of the research was particularly timely, capturing some of the last cohort of students to enter higher education in the United Kingdom, prior to the introduction of tuition fees in 1998. As such, it serves as a benchmark study. However this very uniqueness of sampling opportunity imposed an added time pressure for me, if my study was to reflect this 'Class of '97'.

Their time, my time and real time

Each organisation has its own time rhythm where activities are governed by particular temporal concerns and temporal constraints. However, as someone researching in an educational setting, I was engaging with a field where the complexities of time were 'less visible than those associated with calendars and clocks' (Adam, 1995:69). I was faced with constraints imposed by buzzers and bells, timetables and examination periods, all of which served to determine the fieldwork periods. This became a major concern, I had the opportunity to capture the stages of the choosing process *but* in order to complete the fieldwork, I needed to get in, get on and get out. Such time pressures raise ethical concerns regarding researchers obtaining data by merely using, and so abusing, the participants (Stanley and Wise,

1993; Oakley, 1994). This was an issue which I reflected upon frequently in my field journal, as the research progressed.

As an ESRC funded student, I was conscious of the additional time pressures imposed on me by my Funding Council. The consequences of any time delay on my part could have Institutional as well as personal consequences. As a feminist researcher, I tried to remain alert to the fact that simply *knowing* about values and ethics is not a sufficient basis on which to conduct research (Lenskyj, 1990). However even with such self-conscious acknowledgement I was unprepared for some of the ethical tensions that I encountered in the field. Some of this focused around the 'grey' area of 'informed consent' (Bulmer, 1982; Punch, 1986; Burgess, 1989; Hornsby-Smith, 1993).

Gaining access to schools proved unproblematic and, while a number of researchers in a range of settings, describe how they were monitored by their gatekeepers (Beynon, 1985; Delamont, 1992; Coffey, 1993), this was not an experience I shared. In fact in most cases quite the opposite was true. However, as Dingwell et al. (1980) note, and I was to discover, within the school setting the hierarchies of consent are not always strictly observed. Our structural framework ensures that children and young adults, are marginalised both socially and politically Aldred (1998). As a consequence I found that Head teachers entered into collective agreements with me, on behalf of their pupils. In most of the schools, the staff saw me simply as an additional 'pair of hands', a supply teacher [albeit unpaid] who could take charge of an entire class for my research. Seen as part of 'the group', each pupil was then automatically expected to comply with these arrangements.

The possibility of my research project adding to the disempowerment of young people raised some very serious ethical concerns for me from a feminist standpoint (Stacey, 1988; Stanley and Wise, 1993; Maynard and Purvis, 1994). Clearly as an adult researcher in an educational setting I was not only perceived by the pupils as being socially more powerful, I *was* more powerful. Having gained access to the sites via the gatekeepers, I had access to a number of 'captive' research groups. In addition to which, my position as a researcher provided me with the opportunity both to interpret and represent the data I collected.

I frequently found myself presented with an Assembly Hall containing the entire lower sixth year, (an incredible, if somewhat unnerving, survey opportunity). But how to tackle issues of informed consents and voluntary participation while maintaining control of the group as a whole? Should I risk embarrassing those who didn't want to take part in the survey by asking them to raise their hands? As a 'substitute teacher', the groups were my responsibility and I couldn't allow anyone who didn't want to participate in the research to leave before the end of the period. In addition to this, and with the self-interest of the project to the fore, I recognised that given the opportunity to 'bunk off', most, if not all, of my research subjects would have disappeared. Pragmatically 'captive' participants were better than none.

Originally I had anticipated a more sensitive form of recruitment with student participation during breaks and free periods. Having realised that this was not going to be possible, I achieved a compromise for this dilemma such that, while the pupils were informed on each occasion that I met them of the 'voluntary' nature of their participation, they remained very much a 'captive' population. Having sketched out the main aims of the research and stressed the confidentiality of the study data I handed out questionnaires to every pupil, and then allowed each the option as to whether or not they should complete the forms. The response rate was 96% or greater in each of the schools surveyed. However there is a need to reflect on how much subtle, if unarticulated, researcher, and/or, peer pressure drove this conformity of action.

Researchers are often required to make pragmatic judgements in the field, time pressures and the desire to gather data from a particular population or in a particular research setting forcing the ethical boundaries to become blurred. Good practice can temporarily become tempered by self-interest and we need to be alert to the dangers inherent in such actions.

Cast as an 'expert'

A further ethical dilemma that the novice researcher will quickly encounter is in the management of field relations. As a feminist researcher, I was comfortable with and prepared for reciprocity in my researcher role. Although mindful of the external time pressures, I tried to give time to the respondents and remain alert to their agendas. I disclosed something of my own biography to those I interviewed. I stressed to the pupils and their families the dual nature of my role. At the time of the study, I was a full time research student, but I am also a mother. I have three adult children, who at that time, were, or had recently been, in the situation of choosing a university. I intended that this information should serve two functions. Firstly I hoped that it would act as an initial 'ice breaker' providing a means of introducing both myself and the topic of my research in a framework which would in part, resonate with their own experiences. While I made it clear that I was happy to listen to their concerns, in confidence, and offer general information and advice, I stressed repeatedly, that I was not an 'expert' on higher education, that I had no connections with the Admissions Tutors at any institution, nor was I intending to promote either my own, or any other university. Having said all this of course I recognise and acknowledge that for many of those families that I interviewed, merely by being there, I was perceived as someone who was familiar with and ergo an 'expert on' matters relating to sixth form subjects, course choices and careers counselling in general.

The following sections will discuss the ethical dilemmas and the consequences of such a role with regard to field relationships. It reflects on the extent to which advice should be given, or withheld, and the consequences implicit in either action. It takes, as case studies, two families from the research, in order to highlight the ways in which I was faced with the ethical dilemma of 'getting involved'.

Drowning not waving: Mena's story

This school has really stuffed it up for me as far as choosing is concerned. I *know* that for a fact. I nearly dropped out last year, I was just so fed up with it all.

Mena Hussein was studying 3 A levels, (English, Geography, and Art) and her school was predicting that she could obtain Grade B passes in all three subjects. Her father, a consultant orthopaedic surgeon, is from Iran, her mother, a medical secretary, Welsh. The family had lived abroad for fourteen years during which time Mena and her brother Ben attended 'British and American Schools', mainly in the Middle East. The decision to return to Wales was made to coincide with Mena's beginning her A level studies. Although an affluent middle-class family, their familiarity with the British education system was very limited. Mena's mother had not been to university and her father was educated overseas and his medical qualifications were gained in the USA.

I interviewed the family on a Sunday morning; just one-week before Mena was expected to return her completed UCAS form to the school. At the beginning of the interview, Mena told me she was intending to apply to do a Hotel Management course at a local College of Further Education. She appeared somewhat sulky, uninterested and apathetic about the whole process. Both parents were very unhappy with her choice and this had resulted in numerous heated 'discussions' within the family. Her father, rather quiet and taciturn clearly disapproved and commented that,

> We feel she is going for something, that is not a proper degree. But, more to the point, something well below her ability. That is why I don't think she will be happy.

Her mother was extremely anxious that Mena should be given some sound advice, but unsure as to where this should come from. Throughout the interview, which lasted for almost three hours, Mrs. Hussein was quite emotional, literally wringing her hands at some stages as she told me of her frustration and sense of impotence in terms of her own inability to advise her daughter,

> We didn't know the system here, we tried to find out we did our very best, we really did. ...I thought 'oh well, better to put them in a traditional school'. But now I am here *well* I am so disappointed...I am really. Well how *much trouble* did we have when we first arrived here?

The family were obviously both angry and frustrated with the lack of help they had received from the school and felt that they had been badly let down. The inability to spend time at the beginning of year 12 discussing A level subject choices and their implications in relation to HE courses had engendered a sense of disillusionment with the sixth form which had simply been compounded over time. As Mrs Hussein told me,

> I rang the school and they didn't even want me there to discuss it. That made me feel pretty shut out then. I mean to say how can I advise Mena if I don't know myself? I think they have been *worse than useless,* especially when parents *want* to be interested and *want* the best for their kids. I think they could have spared me ten minutes! Even if it was just to say 'oh well we can't help you, you have to go here or go there'. But they gave me no time, no time what so ever.

The resultant sense of disengagement with the system had allowed for a sense of apathy in Mena. She had 'settled' for a catering option because, in her Saturday job as a waitress at a large hotel in Cardiff, she had met several of the staff who had done this type of course and said it was 'a good laugh'. Mena admitted she was very angry and frustrated with the school because they had not provided her with any real opportunity to discuss her various options. She told me,

The whole thing's just so stressful. It really is. I don't know what I'm doing; I don't have a clue. But the school just *expects* me to be able to deal with it. You know, choose where to go, fill in the form and choose what to do.

Mena was under pressure from the school, to return the UCAS form on time, and from her parents, to consider her choices more fully. Knowing the grades that Mena was capable of achieving, more than mid way into the interview I asked Mena what grades were required to do the catering course she intended applying for. On being told that they were well below her own predicted grades I asked Mena her opinion of pupils in her school who were predicted similar grades, 'were they her among her circle of friends?' 'Did she get on with them?' and her reply was,

I think they are OK, I suppose, well sort of, I mean. But well if you want me to be really honest then I think that they are a bunch of wankers, I don't really like them I suppose. I don't hang around with them, nor have any thing to do with them really.

I then asked her why she intended spending the next three years of her life with such a group when she clearly had such a low opinion of them. Gradually during the remainder of the interview she told me that she would really like to study Law, but felt it was now too late to choose that option. At this point, I self consciously came out of researcher role. I began to offer advice, telling her that she could make a later application through UCAS and suggested that she make contact with some Law Schools and Law students in order to find out about the various law course available.

By the time I left the house the family had worked out a plan of action for the following month. Mena became quite animated about the prospect and the longer we talked, the more enthusiasm she showed for this option. When the interview ended she had decided, with her parents' agreement, that she would take the next few days off school to look into the prospects of applying to study Law. I was concerned about the interview, conscious of the ethical implications of my having overstepped the researcher boundary. However this seemed less important when Mena said,

Well I feel much better now that I have decided to make a decision. It's helped me so much just talking to you because, well, you are not biased. You are not telling me which course you think I should do, or saying oh you should apply here, or there to do this or that. You just let me talk.

My ethical dilemma here was really a case of having crossed the boundary from impartial observer to 'interfering adviser'. This was something I reflected about later in my journal.

> I could see that the 'penny had dropped' when I asked Mena why she was prepared to spend a further three years with they type of people that she seemed to have such a poor opinion of. It was as if the realisation had finally dawned as to some of the 'real' differences there were between courses. She changed visibly before my eyes. Her whole demeanour became more animated, she became enthusiastic about the possibility of researching her options for Law. It was really brilliant!!
> BUT I just hope that this initial momentum is sustained - if that is what *Mena* wants - and that she does go on to apply for Law.
> What is the ethical standpoint here? I couldn't just observe I had to offer some slight? steer.
> BUT - Did I interfere? Or was I merely the catalyst? I *really* hope it was the latter.

The follow up questionnaire survey, conducted in each of the schools and colleges in the study in the Spring of Year 13, provided a list of each university which the pupils had applied to, in their preferred order of choice. I was delighted to see from her questionnaire response that Mena had applied to six universities to study Law and received conditional offers from four, but still conscious of the part I had played and the ethical implications for the research. However, I hadn't fully appreciated the level of my 'involvement' with Mena until it became time to contact the family after the A level results were known, as my journal indicates,

> This is IT - Today I'm phoning the families. I am really nervous about contacting Mena, what if she didn't get the grades she needs to meet her Law offers; will she regret having applied?
> What about my role in all this? I will feel responsible somehow. If I hadn't interviewed them and then intervened what would she have done?
> I need to know the outcome although I'm dreading it in some ways!

I telephoned the Hussein home and spoke to an excited and delighted Mena who had gained the grades necessary to read Law at her chosen university. My journal entry later that day said it all,

> YES!!!!!

> I can't believe how good this feels. If I do nothing else - I have made a difference. She was over the moon and so glad she had made the decision to apply. I have been excited all day - it's just brilliant news.

This feel good factor does not detract from the fact that I may have overstepped the boundary of research. Should my role in the process be seen as an unwarranted 'meddling', an unprofessional breach of the ethical code of practice? Or can such a degree of involvement be justified as reciprocity of time and knowledge in the research process because there was a positive outcome?

Unfortunately, as Marie's story indicates, ethical dilemmas in field relations sometimes result in decisions where the outcomes are not always so positive.

Last of all in the sack race: after the event

Maria Thomas was the eldest of three children. Both parents were long term unemployed with no experience of post compulsory education. Maria was formally registered as a sixth form pupil at one school where she studied A level English. Although her previous local comprehensive did not have a sixth form, she had a good rapport with some of the staff and was studying A level Art there,

When I interviewed the family, it was apparent that this arrangement had resulted in Maria missing out on a lot of the social and pastoral curriculum provided in the sixth form of her new school. Since the two schools are some distance apart, Maria spent considerable parts of the school day walking between the two sites which led to her being absent during registration periods and tutorial sessions when much of the UCAS and other HE information was given out. I spoke to the family in mid October of Year 13, a few weeks before the completed UCAS forms were due to be returned to the school. It became increasingly apparent during the interview that Maria and her parents were clearly confused about the whole application process.

Maria knew that going to university was costly and that financially her family would not be able to support her if she wanted to go away to study. During the interview she told me that if she went on to higher education she would have to study locally and live at home in order to cut down on the costs. The family were unaware of the local authority maintenance grants (which were still available for 1997 entry) or how to go about applying for them, or even how to complete the UCAS form.

It was clear that the family, for whom this was their first engagement with post-compulsory education, felt totally out of their depth. Although very proud of their daughter and anxious to encourage her, they were unable to offer any practical help or financial support. They were relying on the school to help Maria through the choice process. As Mrs Thomas told me,

> We don't have a clue really, no idea at all how you are meant to go about it all. I tried reading through some of them forms, but well you need a degree to make sense of them, you really do.

At the end of the interview I spent about an hour with the family, during which time I gave them copies of the student grant and loan literature, none of which they had seen before. I also talked through the various stages of the UCAS application procedure with Maria and suggested that she try to make an appointment with her school tutor for a mutually convenient time when they could discuss her course options. I gave what practical guidance I could but, when I left, it was with the sense that the family was still very unclear about the whole process and that they were particularly uneasy about the costs associated with higher education. I wondered if I should have done more and reflected on this later in my research journal,

> I think that the Thomas family are probably the most confused people that I have spoken to. Tomorrow I'll send them the address of the local Careers Office and their booklet on applying to university.
> Maria is really missing out because of this odd situation of being between schools.
> I don't know if I should call back and offer to help her fill out the form.
> BUT that is *really* intervening - ethically not on. AND do I have the time?
> I think I have done what I can, I just hope it works out for her.

Unfortunately, it did not work out for Maria. I later found out from discussion with her teachers and with her parents, that by the time she did see her tutor she was told she had missed the UCAS deadline and would be required to submit a late application. Lacking any clear guidance from the school and home, and lacking the confidence to be proactive in seeking help, she decided not to apply for a university place. Nevertheless, she gained grade C passes in both her English and her Art 'A' level examinations. The equivalent of 12 points, sufficient to allow her entry to higher education on a number of courses in several of the university institutes in the region. The entry in my field journal reads;

I feel really angry at the way in which Maria has been let down. But if I'm honest, I'm also feeling guilty that *I* didn't do more to help.
Could I have done something? and really more to the point *should* I have? I was anxious about the ethics of interfering, but also concerned about the time aspect of the project and my need to get on with my data collection.
Maria has done well. It's a brilliant result but seems to have passed largely without comment as far as the schools are concerned. And as far as she is concerned - what now?

I felt, and continue to feel, a sense of regret and some shame that I did not do more to help Maria. Yet I recognise that I was then, and am now a qualitative researcher, and as such need to be bound by a code of ethics designed to protect the participants in research from the meddling of well meaning amateurs. I was neither an admissions tutor, nor a career advisor, rather my role was to make visible the social by means of description, which as Bourdieu (1990) notes 'is in itself a critical force'. This I feel must be the overriding aim of the researcher.

Conclusions

Delamont (1992) notes that most researchers say little about leaving the field, other than to record their exit. Leaving the field, especially if things have gone well is difficult. Letting go becomes almost as much of a challenge as getting in. One of the issues germane to the entire process is that of the ethical nature of the research. I spent two years researching this cohort of pupils. I shared the excitement of some and the frustrations and disappointments of others. Their lived realities provide the data, which serve to tell this story. Fieldwork confronts the researcher with a range of ethical dilemmas, many demanding immediate responses. Decisions, once taken, cannot be revoked but may have far reaching implications for those who participate in the research process.
The increasing demands on, and from Funding Councils, will surely exacerbate strictures on research time. Such constraints will impact on researchers forced to confront issues of research design and practice. These should not, indeed must not allow for the 'cutting of corners' as far as the ethics of the research process are concerned. Reading accounts of researching the social may alert us to the ethical dilemmas, the perils and the pitfalls that are entailed. However qualitative research demands a rite of passage, and decisions taken in the field will have consequences that may well be cause for celebration or regret in the years that follow.

References

Adam, B. (1995) *Timewatch*. Cambridge: Polity.

Aldred, P. (1998) Ethnography and Discourse Analysis: Dilemmas in Representing the Voices of Children in J. Ribbens, and R. Edwards (Eds). *Feminist Dilemmas in Qualitative Research: Public Knowledge and Private Lives*. London: Sage.

Ball, S.J. (1981) *Beachside Comprehensive: a case study of secondary schooling*. Cambridge: Cambridge University Press.

Beynon, J. (1985) *Initial Encounters in the Secondary School*. London: Falmer.

Bourdieu, P. and Passeron, J-C. (1990) (2nd Edition). *Reproduction in Education, Society and Culture*. London: Sage.

Bulmer, M. (1982) *Social Research Ethics*. London: Macmillan.

Burgess, R.G. (1989) (Ed). *The Ethics of Educational Research*. London: Falmer Press.

Burgess, R.G. (1984) *Experiencing Comprehensive Education : a study of Bishop McGregor School*. London: Methuen.

Burman, E. (1994) *Deconstructing Developmental Psychology*. London: Routledge.

Coffey, A. (1993) *Double Entry: The professional and organisational socialisation of graduate accountants*. Unpublished PhD Thesis. University of Wales: Cardiff.

Connell, R.W., Ashenden, D.J., Kessler, S. and Dowsett, G.W. (1982) *Making the Difference. Schools, Families and Social Divisions*. London: George Allen and Unwin.

Delamont, S. (1992) *Fieldwork in Educational Settings*. London: Falmer.

Dingwall, R., Payne, G. and Payne, L. (1980) *The development of ethnography in Britain*. Oxford: Centre for Socio-Legal Studies.

Hammersley, M. and Atkinson, P. (1995) (2nd Edition). *Ethnography Principles in Practice*. London: Routledge.

Hornsby-Smith, M. (1993) Gaining Access in N. Gilbert. (Ed). *Researching Social Life*. London: Sage.

Lensky, H. (1990). Beyond plumbing and prevention. A feminist approach to sex education. *Gender and Education*. Vol.2(2) pp. 217-230.

Maynard, M. and Purvis, J. (1994) (Eds.) *Researching Women's Lives from a Feminist Perspective*. London: Taylor and Francis.

Oakley, A. (1981) Interviewing Women: a contradiction in terms. In H. Roberts (Ed). *Doing Feminist Research*. London: Routledge and Kegan Paul.

Oakley, A. (1994) 'Women and children first and last: parallels and differences between children's and women's studies'. In B. Mayall (Ed). *Children's Childhoods Observed and Experienced*. London: Falmer Press.

Pugsley, L. (1998) *Class of '97: Higher Education Markets and Choice*. Unpublished PhD Thesis: Cardiff University of Wales.

Punch, M. (1986) *The Politics and Ethics of Fieldwork*. London: Sage.

Rose, N. (1985) *The Psychological Complex*. London: Routledge.

Stacey, J. (1988) Can there be a feminist ethnography? *Women's Studies International Forum*. Vol.1(1) pp. 21-27.

Stanley, L. and Wise, S. (1993) *Breaking Out Again: feminist ontology and epistemology*. London: Routledge.

3 They told me I couldn't do that: ethical issues of intervention in careers education and guidance research

PATRICK WHITE

Introduction

Although by its very nature a contested area, writers in the area of ethical research seem to have reached a consensus on one particular issue: that it is important both to share experience of fieldwork with the wider research community and to keep the issues surrounding the ethics of social scientific research the subject of a live and continually evolving debate. Bell and Newby (1977:9-10) argue that accounts of research experiences are as, if not more, valuable for learning than most methods textbooks, whilst Helen Roberts (1981:1) contends that 'problems raised in personal accounts of research are themselves of sociological importance'. Burgess (1984:207) urges 'constant self-evaluation and reflection' of research experiences on the part of researchers in order to confront and understand 'the moral dilemmas and the compromises' which have to be made in the conduct of social research. Hammersley and Atkinson (1995:285), more recently, call for public discussion of ethical issues in order to stimulate the deliberations of individuals and teams involved in the practice of research.

It is as a contribution to this kind of discussion that this chapter is written, hoping it may provide a basis for further discussion and that the experiences it describes might provide 'intellectual stimulus' for the contemporary research community. The rationale presented represents only one 'solution' to a particular set of ethical dilemmas which were experienced during one particular research project. Different circumstances will necessarily call for different approaches. It is hoped, however, that the rationale provided will be examined by interested readers and either be accepted as a suitable rationale for future practice or provoke further discussion of ethical conduct in social research. For as the commentators above infer, researchers will be better prepared to make decisions regarding their own conduct when they are made aware of the experiences of others.

Interviews, interviewing and ethics

Interviewing is a form of social interaction. However, the exact nature of the social interaction that an interview constitutes has been the subject of debate. Obviously, the 'interview' can take many different forms and this will dictate, to a large extent, what kind of interaction can or cannot take place within its parameters. Nevertheless, given a particular 'interview situation', the behaviour of both interviewer and interviewee necessarily combine to dictate the nature of the relationship that develops, and which in turn shapes the eventual form the interview takes. The traditional textbook paradigm of 'interviewer detachment', in which the interviewer both actively seeks to control and depersonalise the interview situation, has been problematised by feminist researchers such as Ann Oakley (1981:41) who argues firstly on the grounds of methodological validity that:

> In most cases, the goal of finding out about people through interviewing is best achieved when the relationship of interviewer and interviewee is not hierarchical and when the interviewer is prepared to invest his or her own personal identity in the relationship.

Roberts (1981) highlights Oakley's commitment to 'reciprocity' in the interview situation and also her critique of the interview as a 'one-way' process. According to Roberts, 'Oakley illustrates the absurdity of this situation through a discussion of the questions her respondents 'asked back' (p.30). Oakley (1981:49) justifies her decision regarding active and involved responses to interviewees' questions both as a political and ethical decision and also in terms of methodological utility, as refusal to give feedback hinders the successful building of 'rapport'. She contrasts her approach with the traditional reliance on 'strategies of avoidance' suggested by many textbooks as useful devices which can be employed to parry questions raised by interviewees (Oakley, 1981:35).

Whilst agreeing with Oakley in terms of both her ethical concerns regarding interviewing and also the value of her approach in terms of conducting 'good' qualitative research, it is necessary to make some qualifications to her approach. The nature of the research she uses to exemplify her viewpoint, both in terms of methodology and subject matter, are ideally suited to fully realise her methodological and ethical aims and as such raise relatively few problems for her (although some criticisms of her paper will be discussed in greater detail below). Indeed, she does acknowledge that 'common sense would suggest that an ethic of detachment on the interviewer's part is much easier to maintain where there is only one meeting with the interviewee' (p.35). This proposition can fairly easily be extended with the further qualification that the shorter the time allocated for the interview, the less chance there is to build enough rapport to establish the type of relationship with the interviewee Oakley advocates. Indeed, in many situations such an 'ethic of detachment' is an almost inevitable consequence of the constraints of time. Oakely's interviews with pregnant mothers averaged a total of 9.4 hours with each interviewee over the course of several meetings (Oakley, 1981:43). This amount of contact time certainly provides an opportunity to 'get acquainted' with an interviewee to the point of 'personalising' the interview situation. However, this situation is not common in contemporary research outside of ethnographic case studies. The majority of interview situations do not fall into this category and are located somewhere on a continuum between the contact time Oakley was granted and the face-to-face administration of short questionnaires. The interviewer can find him- or herself faced with temporal limitations which severely restrict the amount of rapport which can be established. It is also the case that many research questions do not require interviews of such a protracted length. For whatever reason 'shorter' interviews are used, they remain fundamentally different in nature as a social situation. The expected behaviour of both interviewer and interviewee is therefore different.

The interview as social interaction

Bok (1982:179) states that 'scientific enquiry ... has to be judged by standards common to other undertakings'. Researchers should not be exempt from 'ordinary restrictions on action' and should utilise the same rules in research situations as they would in everyday life (Bok, 1982:179). In applying this argument to the research interview it can be concluded that Oakley, considering the nature of her methodology, behaved appropriately. In over 9 hours of contact time, it would be artificial (and perhaps impossible) to attempt to avoid any personal investment and reciprocity in the interview situation. Oakley's accounts of 'the transition to friendship'

(1981:44-46) would seem to be a reasonably expected outcome given the length of time she spent with participants. However, as noted above, many (perhaps most) interview situations involve considerably less contact time between interviewer and interviewee. With shorter interview contact time the relationship between interviewer and interviewee could be reasonably expected only to develop to the stage of becoming 'acquaintances', and the two parties may even remain as comparative 'strangers'. Following Bok's principle of applying the same rules of behaviour to research as one would for everyday social interaction, the behaviour that would be possible, or even *appropriate*, in the interview situation would change according to the dictates of time. Different social norms apply when talking to a 'stranger', an 'acquaintance' and a 'friend' and these will inevitably affect the behaviour that is expected in different interview situations. Attempting personal disclosure and adopting a counselling role in a 20 minute interview would not only be inappropriate and disconcerting to the interviewee, but would in fact be impossible to achieve with any degree of success in such short time. It could also limit the possibilities of collecting any useful data and render the interview an unfulfilling experience for both interviewer and interviewee. This is, of course, an extreme example, but is used here to illustrate that the natural constraints imposed by time are not always within the control of the researcher whatever his or her preferred research strategy or methodological approach.

The politics of the research process: considerations 'outside' the interview context

A final qualification to Oakley's proposals regards the politics of the research process. These operate at many levels, apply differently in different areas of research and are omnipresent in not only the research process itself, but also in the publication of research findings (see: Punch, 1985).

Every researcher has commitments which he or she must fulfil as part of a 'research bargain'. Whilst Oakley only articulates these commitments in terms of her responsibilities to those being interviewed, they usually extend much further. In much educational research elements of the research bargain can be traced from the students, through staff, headteachers, and finally to the university department and organisation sponsoring the research project. Social scientists in areas other than education doubtless face similar situations. All involved parties stipulate conditions which have to be fulfilled in order for the research to continue and each group's requirements may have direct or indirect implications for a research strategy. Some of these requirements may also appear to be conflicting. In addition, the researcher or research team also invest a great deal of themselves in a particular project and the successful completion or non-completion of that project can have long-term implications for their personal career biographies and the institution they represent. The ethical considerations of the researcher to him/herself cannot be ignored or sidelined. Whilst Oakley (1981:40) argues that 'what is good for interviewers is not necessarily good for interviewees', the reverse is also true.

Commitments researchers have to funding agencies and academic departments do not need to be spelled out here. They are a familiar aspect of most researchers' daily lives. Punch (1985) gives a detailed account of some of the problems which can arise. In educational research, as in many other areas, researchers operate at many levels, for example requesting the participation of staff and making negotiations for access at the institutional level. The very nature of these procedures give rise to commitments to different groups of individuals at different levels of the institutional hierarchy. Such commitments will differ in form according to the positions of the individuals involved, their role within the institution and their corresponding interests. Social scientific investigations into educational reforms or curricula are often mistakenly (and sometimes suspiciously) regarded by 'gatekeepers' as evaluative in nature. And as Becker (1967: 244) warns, 'superordinate groups ... will be sensitive to the implications of our work'. Helen Simons (1988:114) expresses similar concerns:

> Even research that is not specifically linked to action is likely to be scrutinised for its relevance to and implications for policy. Our subjects know that, and are sensitive to any possibility of advantage or disadvantage that may ensue as a consequence of their collaboration.

Negotiating access is thus a particularly sensitive process. But access also brings with it further responsibilities. For example, participating institutions sometimes request reports about their policies or practice. These are often offered in advance by research teams keen to offer an incentive to prospective participants. Staff who have been closely involved with the research (and who sometimes have given their own time to aid the researcher) anxiously await this source of feedback from an established research institution. The production of these reports is itself a political process, as researchers must not proffer inaccurate information, but should also be aware of 'spoiling the field' for their colleagues. Here again, loyalties are split between the researchers and the researched.

Such reports, however, are by no means the only part of the research bargain. There are usually other factors which have been agreed either implicitly or explicitly during access negotiations. For many reasons, interviews with students, for example, are more usually arranged through institutions and staff than directly through parents. Researchers must consider their conduct not merely in relation to students (even if they are the only participants *directly* involved in the research), but also to staff and institutions who have co-operated. As mentioned earlier, staff (sometimes delegated by senior colleagues) helping researchers operationalise their research plan often invest a great deal in a particular research project. They are also frequently involved in research interviews themselves, as well as allowing observation of their teaching, and so on. It is important not to engage in any kind of 'reciprocity' with students (and for that matter staff) which may compromise the participating institution or any members of its staff in any way. 'Reciprocity' with students during interviews may be particularly volatile in this respect, as could many other forms of intervention, as the possibility of undermining staff or institutional authority is ever-present. As Alison Kelly (1985:103) points out, even in action research studies she was involved in, the 'right to take action was dependent on negotiation'. In other areas of investigation outside the realm of action research this right is seldom negotiated before entry to the field. In many cases it probably would not be granted to researchers requesting it.

The political nature of knowledge

During her fieldwork interviews Oakley's (1982) concern was providing women with information and advice that they had felt unable to ask their doctor. This was either of a practical nature or concerned Oakley's own experiences and was at the request of the participants. However, information in other contexts can differ in important and problematic ways. Firstly, the researcher must consider whether he or she is qualified to respond to the question being asked. It seems clear that Oakley felt confident in this respect. Secondly, there is a distinctly *political* nature to information and 'knowledge' in any context, and even personal experience is necessarily 'partial'. To intervene in the provision of information and advice, itself a political action, *could* be justified if the researcher was well qualified and informed in the relevant area, but arguably does not constitute appropriate behaviour for an interested academic. It also risks undermining the professionals working with participants and engendering conflict between previously harmonious parties. Oakley did not problematise the political nature of the information and advice which she gave in her interviews. Whilst dedicating the first part of her paper to a critique of the ideological basis of the traditional, 'masculine' methodological paradigm of positivism, she does not discuss the more obvious issues surrounding the ideological basis of medical knowledge (see: Wright and Treacher (1982) for a full discussion of this issue). Although she may have seen some of the information or advice she gave as apolitical (outside of her concern for the women she studied and women as a group), this position can be disputed. She attempts to separate the types of questions she was asked by interviewees into four distinct categories (1982:42-43) but in doing so fails to acknowledge that there may be no clear division between 'advice', 'information' and 'personal experiences'. Her criteria for intervention, based around these different categories of data, thus begins to break down. The irony of breaking down the questions in this way (which does little in terms of substantiating or clarifying her arguments) is that she presents her data and analysis in a form characteristic of the 'positivist approach' she is so critical of. This approach, used in other research, could be seen as using the tools of analysis that best suit the data, and so be commended as good social scientific practice. But in this particular example she is also guilty of creating categories which over-simplify the reality of the situation she is studying, a criticism more frequently aimed at research employing the 'positivist' methods of analysis she denounces.

An additional objection is that there could be unforeseen future consequences for an individual which may be more harmful than the benefits bestowed by the initial advice or intervention. Bok (1978:178) cautions that:

> in much research, there is neither … clear abuse nor such obvious innocuousness. The risks, their magnitude and probability, may be unknown or disputed. *The benefits hoped for are just as conjected.* [emphasis added]

Shils (1982:134) also alerts us that 'the real and immediate benefits which [research] can bring are … small and problematic'. Although both these writers are referring to balance of costs and benefits of research in the longer term, their warning can also be applied effectively to the proposed benefits of intervention whilst *still in the field*. Kelly (1985:104), discussing her experience of intervention in action research finds that 'our intentions, and high ethical principles of benefiting children, may not be realised in practice'. Hammersley and Atkinson (1995:279) express a similar view:

> Sometimes actions that are motivated by ethical ideals can cause severe problems, not just for researcher but for the people they are studying as well.

Also, although intervention may be justified in terms of an individual's well-being, there could be serious ramifications if any un-negotiated intervention is by those higher up in the institutional hierarchy who were involved in granting initial access. These could affect the individual concerned, who still has to study or work in that institution, but may also have implications for the future of a research project.

Limits to reciprocity

This is not to say, however, that participants involved in fieldwork interviews find the experience completely sterile. Such interviews can provide participants with the opportunity to talk about their professional or personal life with someone outside of the institution they are situated in or the social sphere they usually inhabit. The researcher's role as a 'therapeutic listener' (Oakley, 1982:51) can give participants a chance reflect on their situation which they may not be afforded in their daily routine. Janet Finch (1993:168) writes of

> instances which demonstrate a feeling which was very common among the women I interviewed ... They (often unexpectedly) had found this kind of interview a welcome experience, in contrast with the lack of opportunities to talk about themselves in this way in other circumstances.

Although in her paper Finch focuses on women who may particularly welcome interviews due to their marginal and isolated position in social and economic life, it could be argued that many other participants in social scientific research have welcomed the interest of a researcher in particular aspects of their lives. It is important to qualify this in one important respect, however. The same restraints which may prohibit or limit 'intimacy and reciprocity' will also devalue the interview as a forum for interviewees to talk through their concerns. The value of such an experience will also differ for each interviewee. Hammersley and Atkinson (1995:283) concur that:

> while there are potential benefits from research for participants, for instance, the chance to talk at length to someone about one's problems, how valuable these are found may vary.

Despite such reservations, it is clear, however, that for many participants social scientific research, especially interviews, may have in Finch's (1993:169) words, 'welcomed the opportunity to try to make sense of some of the contradictions in their lives in the presence of a sympathetic listener'. Researchers should not feel that they can only contribute to their participants' welfare by directly intervening in their lives, or via their distant and intangible contribution to a body of knowledge, but must realise that their research is often a welcome opportunity and stimulus for those involved as participants to reflect on their own experiences. Social scientists can thus, in their deliberation of ethical conduct in the field, at least feel some consolation in this knowledge.

References

Becker, H.S. (1967) 'Who's Side Are We on?', in *Social Problems* 14 (3): 329-347.

Bell, C. and Newby, H. (eds.) (1977) *Doing Sociological Research*. London: Allen and Unwin.

Bok, S. (1982) 'Freedom and Risk', in M. Bulmer (ed.) *Social Research Ethics*. London: Macmillan.

Burgess, R.G. (1984) *In the Field: An Introduction to Field Research*. London: Unwin Hyman.

Burgess, R.G. (1989) 'Grey Areas: Ethical Dilemmas in Educational Ethnography', in R.G. Burgess (ed.) *The Ethics of Educational Research*. London: Falmer Press.

Finch, J. (1993) 'It's Great to have Someone to Talk to: Ethics and Politics of Interviewing Women', in M. Hammersley (ed.) *Social Research: Philosophy, Politics and Practice*. London: Sage.

Hammersley, M. and Atkinson, P. (1995) *Ethnography: Principles in Practice*. London: Routledge.

Kelly, A. (1982) 'Action Research: What Is It and What Can it Do?', in R.G. Burgess (ed.) *Issues in Educational Research: Qualitative Research*. London: Falmer Press.

Oakley, A. (1981) 'Interviewing Women: A Contradiction in Terms', in H. Roberts *Doing Feminist Research*. London: Routledge and Kegan Paul.

Punch, M. (1985) *The Politics and Ethics of Fieldwork*. Sage University Paper on Qualatative Research Methods (Vol. 3). Beverley Hills: Sage.

Roberts, H. (ed.) (1981) *Doing Feminist Research*. London: Routledge and Kegan Paul.

Shils, E. (1982) 'Social Inquiry and the Autonomy of the Individual', in M. Bulmer (ed.) *Social Research Ethics*. London: Macmillan.

Simons, H. (1988) 'The Ethics of Case Study Research and Evaluation', in R. Burgess (ed.) *The Ethics of Social Research*. Lewes: Falmer Press.

Wright, P. and Treacher, A. (eds.) (1992) *The Problem of Medical Knowledge: examining the social construction of medicine*. Edinburgh: University of Edinburgh Press.

4 Telling tales on technology: the ethical dilemmas of critically researching educational computing

NEIL SELWYN

Introduction

The last three decades have left many people convinced of the centrality of the computer to society's lurch into the twenty-first century. Fitting in neatly with visions of a post-industrial, 'information society' the development of the computer has been heralded as the epitome of 'progress'; reinforcing a belief in technologically-induced advancement rooted in the Enlightenment (Marx, 1987). Computers are also seen as a 'seductive technology' (Kling, 1996) or, more accurately, the centrepiece of seductive visions and expectations. This seduction is primarily rooted in the endless possibilities apparently achievable by all at relatively low cost and little effort. In this way, societal trust in information and communications technology (ICT) has tended to be couched in very modernist, rational terms. As Kitchin (1998, p.57) concludes, 'the basic tenet is that we will use technology to progress and that potentialities will be realised simply because they are possible'.

It is perhaps unsurprising that many educationalists have been infused by an unerring trust in the computer. Indeed, it has long been received wisdom that the use of computers in education is inherently a 'good thing'. This stems from deeply-held anticipation amongst influential elements of the educational community that the integration of the computer into schools will have a fundamental and irreversible influence on learning and teaching processes. Over thirty years ago, Suppes (1966) reasoned that the flexibility and interactive nature of the computer would have an almost immediate and permanent effect on the educational process. Two decades later this claim was echoed by Seymour Papert (1980) who, from a Piagetian perspective, argued that forging new relationships between computers and humans would result in 'a future where the computer will be a significant part of

42

every child's life' (Papert 1980, p.18) and that schools, as a result, will be obsolete (Papert 1995). Other authors have enthusiastically echoed these claims to the point where Stonier and Conlin (1985, p.10) could assume that:

[T]he entire educational system will begin to revolve increasingly around the computer. Combined with teachers and parents, books and classrooms, the system over the next few decades will change. At the core of it will be the computer.

Thus ICT has proved unique in educational terms in that, unlike any other innovation, its benefit to schools and colleges has remained largely unchallenged, quickly becoming an established educational orthodoxy (Robins and Webster, 1989). Against such consensual optimism the prospect of questioning the rationality of educational computing would appear to be unproductive and churlish.

The need to tell tales on educational technology: challenging the techno-utopic orthodoxy

As Langdon Winner (1993) asserts, the bulk of technological change has occurred in a social and intellectual vacuum - and it would seem that educational technology has been no different. Since the computer's introduction into the classroom, academic research into educational ICT has tended to uncritically reflect societal faith in technology. Whilst a positive approach towards technology is not in itself a disadvantage, educational computing research has continually been limited by an *excessive* optimism and technophilia. Although a succession of authors have attempted to point out these fundamental shortcomings (e.g. Beynon and Mackay, 1989; Kenway, 1996; Young, 1984) most educational computing research is still characterised by an underlying distrust and avoidance of theory coupled with an unwillingness to consider the social, political, cultural and economic aspects of ICT in schools. As Kenway (1996) concludes, social science research in this area has been too 'micro-focused', with a 'wilful blindness' to the social and cultural contexts and wider implications of technology. To compound this problem, educational computing studies have distanced themselves from the rest of social science research over the last decade by exhibiting an almost overt distrust of qualitative methods. Against this background, the present chapter presents a personal account of the ethical dilemmas encountered when adopting a more questioning, qualitative approach to researching (and reporting on) the state of educational computing in UK schools and colleges.

Faced with designing a research project focusing on educational use of ICT the need to adopt a more critical approach became quickly apparent. On a purely personal level, as I began to feel my way around the relevant literature very little of the optimistic rhetoric therein resonated with my own experiences of educational ICT use; whether in compulsory or post-compulsory settings. Furthermore, the bulk of education technology literature I came across failed to reflect, or even acknowledge, the bleak picture of schools' ICT use as painted by countless 'official' government and inspectorate reports. I found myself reading numerous accounts of the potential benefits of using 'virtual reality' and 'hypermedia' in the classroom in the same breath as official statistics were telling me that the majority of computers in schools at the time were incapable of running Microsoft Windows - let alone sophisticated multimedia applications. The earlier warnings from the likes of Beynon, Mackay, Kenway et al. could not, it seems, have fallen on deafer ears. It was from this basis that I began to construct my own research project.

Echoing Qvortrup's (1984, p.7) argument that computing 'cannot be properly understood if we persist in treating technology and society as two independent entities', I strove to move the research project beyond the view that educational computing is distinct from society in either its cause or effect. Instead I made a conscious effort to eschew the positions of either technological determinism or 'techno-neutralism' and move towards a perspective that avoids drawing a 'technology'/'society' distinction and, instead, focused on the *social contexts* where technologies are used (Bromley, 1997). Yet, in doing so I quickly found myself at odds both with the closed culture of educational practice I sought to examine and the academic body of knowledge I ultimately sought to position my findings in; raising a number of unforeseen and unexpected ethical considerations. It is this struggle that the remainder of this chapter reflects on - how to 'tell tales' on a technology as deified as the computer in education and make your voice(s) heard.

The research project: the permeation of information technology into 16-19 education

The two and a half year project sought to examine the use of ICT in full-time 16 to 19 education in Welsh schools and colleges (i.e. 'Sixth Form' and 'Further' education spanning Grades 12 to 14). Despite the burgeoning significance of the 16-19 sector in the UK the use of ICT in this phase of education had tended to be overlooked by previous researchers, leaving my project starting from somewhat of an empirical wilderness. Because of this, it was decided to split the project into two distinct phases - an initial 'quantitative' phase to map out a preliminary 'snapshot' of ICT use in the sector which could then be used to inform the second phase of qualitative research - designed to unpack and extend the trends highlighted from the quantitative data. It is this latter phase of qualitative investigation that this chapter will concern itself with.

In particular this chapter will explore the ethical problems that arose in qualitatively examining such a closed area of education and the subesequnt dissemination of findings back to a traditionally 'techno-utopic' educational community. Aside from more 'conventional' ethical problems encountered when carrying out qualitative research in educational settings (for example see White in this volume), an unexpected element of ethical 'ambiguity' was particularly prominent in 'pre' and 'post' data-collection contexts; both in terms of negotiating access to participants and, then, disseminating the findings back to stakeholders.

Emerging motivations

Schools and colleges understandably resent being seen as 'research fodder' and more often than not negotiate a 'research bargain' aimed at advantaging them as well as the researcher (Hammersley and Atkinson, 1995). As Phtiaka (1994) reiterates, the question of 'what's in it for us?' is now of paramount importance to educational institutions when negotiating participation in research projects and often extends beyond general reports of the research findings to demands for more 'market-sensitive', school-specific feedback. Although this had not been immediately apparent when negotiating access for my research it slowly emerged as the project wore on. In anticipation of the schools demanding some form of 'payback' I had initially made vague illusions to writing up a report of my findings if the schools so requested - deciding to wait upon the weight of demand before finally deciding what form this should take. Despite foreseeing the need for some form of feedback at the end of the project I was soon taken aback by the ferocity of some of the institutions' desire for this privy information and, more importantly, how this eventually shaped their reaction and reading of the data.

Throughout the fieldwork I was constantly approached for reassurance that a report would be forthcoming which would crucially include details of other schools' situations. This, to an extent, reflected the general lack of co-operation between institutions in the area. One ICT Co-ordinator was very keen for me to recount even the basic levels of provision in other schools as he had no legitimate means of discovering himself. My role was clearly reversed in this situation to being *his* 'key informant'. Indeed, in most cases, the desire for knowledge was of a distinctly competitive nature.

As the project progressed schools became more open about their motivations for participating. The more competitive institutions wished to confirm their advantage whilst the less 'well-endowed' wanted 'ammunition' to press their governing bodies for extra investment in ICT. Thus, it was quickly apparent that the recent 'marketisation' of post-16 education had forced institutions to make a commitment to ICT in terms of the educational marketplace and their ability to compete for students. As this college ICT co-ordinator argued;

> One of the things that we're always saying is look, we've got to get our IT facilities sorted. Because when kids come from schools they're going to come from a background where they've got lots of dinky equipment. So the facilities that we've got here in college have got to be at least as good, if not better, than the facilities in schools otherwise it'll be 'why go to [the FE] College? The hardware is out of date. The machines are far too slow'. Its a sexy thing at the moment to have [College ICT Co-ordinator, July 1997].

In response to this I decided that the quantitative section of the reports would include composite data for the school sixth form and college sectors, neatly avoiding any breach of confidentiality between schools. Yet upon presenting the data back to institutions the conditions of my research were quickly defined as much more than was made apparent during the laissez-faire introductory encounters.

Disseminating the data

Once the fieldwork period was over I had to decide how to disseminate my findings, especially in light of the institutions' explicit wishes for detailed market-driven feedback. Indeed, as Hodkinson and Sparkes (1993, p.125) contend, one of the core ethical problems facing the researcher in this situation is what nature the school-specific feedback should take; in simple terms 'what to feed back to whom'. Seeking a period of grace, I decided to wait until the data had been analysed before arriving at a decision.

It quickly become apparent that, in general terms, the conclusions of the study may not be as positive as some of the institutions had perhaps hoped. The study was reaching several conclusions. Primarily, the level and nature of ICT use in 16-19 education was extremely sporadic and heavily shaped by students' qualification pathways and subject areas. The findings painted an overall picture of educational computing being very much shaped by the cultures and contexts that surround its use with only a restricted sub-culture of 'high-ICT' students and staff making any sustained and extensive use of computers. Moreover, the interview data suggested that the rationales behind students' rejection of educational computing were often more to do with school-based factors than an 'inability' or 'deficiency' to use ICT. Although a sizeable minority of students felt unable to use computers effectively, a noticeable number of students also saw ICT as wholly inappropriate to the nature of their work and therefore chose not to use it actively. A further section of students also viewed computers and computer users with a disdain and even stigma which also precluded them using ICT in school and college. On the whole, teaching staff also felt constrained by the pressures of qualification pathways, especially the emphasis throughout the A-level curriculum on the final examination, rather than extraneous 'extra-curricular' activities such as ICT.

So, having successfully completed the supposedly hardest part of the research process (that of gathering the data) the project was faced with a potentially bigger challenge: how was it best to present this critical reading of educational computing to the institutions concerned? As Hodkinson and Sparkes (1993) argue, at the crux of this 'dilemma of dissemination' is what the researcher hopes to achieve by feeding back data to participants. Simply trying to 'tell it like it is' and disowning yourself from any consequences may lead to as many dangers and unethical problems as it seeks to avoid. Yet, in settling on an approach I had to be clear as to *what* the project was trying to achieve; Increased equity of access to ICT? Improved facilities?

Moreover, *who* was the project seeking to empower or aid? The students themselves; their subject teachers; ICT co-ordinators; senior management teams? As Hodkinson and Sparkes (1993, p.127) conclude, 'any such decision predetermines the nature of what we feedback, the way in which it is done and to whom'.

In the end it was decided to produce a short twenty page report summarising the specific quantitative and qualitative data for each institution with the qualitative section taking the form of aggregated student data encompassing five of the recurrent themes of the study: area of study, qualification, gender, access and teaching staff. The use of a report as part of the research bargain is now common practice in educational research (Burgess 1983, Simons 1987) but still raises ethical concern of what to feedback to schools and internal confidentiality. In this way, to preserve the integrity and anonymity of my sources, it also was clear that feedback would have to be restricted to student data as the limited number of staff members interviewed would leave many of them instantly recognisable to their colleagues and senior management (Riddell 1989).

i) Feeding back the reports to ICT co-ordinators

Throughout the feedback process I was very aware of preserving the 'fragile' and 'provisional' triangle of trust between researcher, senior management and teaching staff (Simons, 1989), and aware that, despite their acquiescence with the carrying out of focus-group interviews, many of the ICT co-ordinators may not have necessarily expected a report based on qualitative data. Nevertheless, keen that the students' 'voices' were heard, I persevered.

Upon presentation, all the ICT co-ordinators received the reports eagerly and generally seemed enthusiastic about the broad-level quantitative data. However, upon reaching the interview sections of the reports the mood of some noticeably changed, with the ICT co-ordinators readily accepting the quantitative findings (however damning) but questioning, challenging or dismissing the interview data as 'not representative' and 'just the students' opinion'. In one case, a college ICT co-ordinator dismissed the entire qualitative section because it was raising issues that had 'not been found in the survey'. Thus in some, but not all, cases there was a clear unwillingness to believe students' voices as readily as trust was put in the quantitative data which in many ways were only cruder summaries of students' opinions and perceptions! The tendency among educators to see quantitative data as providing 'the facts' and, therefore qualitative data as almost irrelevant is well documented (Finch, 1985; Burgess, 1985) and, therefore, was not in itself that surprising. However, the subsequent (mis)application of the qualitative findings by the institutions was as telling as the initial disinterest.

Revisiting the research sites a few weeks after the feedback sessions, it was soon apparent that virtually the only finding that the senior management teams and ICT co-ordinators had picked up from the qualitative data was a sub-section of the report on students' complaints concerning lack of teacher awareness of computers. This in itself was only one element of a much larger analysis which highlighted many perceived shortcomings concerning the provision, resourcing and organisation of ICT in the schools as well as a lack of curricular commitment and importance. Yet, despite these many other salient points the one factor constantly focused on was students' views of apparent staff deficiencies. One institution went as far as circulating a leaflet after the project to members of staff proclaiming that 'the one main finding' of my project was a 'lack of skill and knowledge amongst staff' and thus urging them to attend ICT training sessions. As Phtiaka (1994) argues, one of the principal disadvantages of offering written feedback is that data may be taken out of context or used for unintended purposes. Nevertheless, the lack of attention paid to the overall qualitative picture was disappointing and at worst distorting the perception of the project among those who had participated. However, such a reaction to the qualitative findings proved to be just a prelude.

ii) Feeding back to the 'ICT committee'

One of the most helpful and amenable institutions had asked whether it would be possible for me to address my findings to their newly established 'Information and Learning Technologies' working party - consisting of staff members from across all departments. This was to be an 'informal meeting' after college hours designed to hopefully give the committee 'food-for-thought' for the rest of the term. Despite the slightly foreboding atmosphere the evening started well enough and my initial presentation of the quantitative data was politely received.

However, once the presentation progressed onto the data collected from the interview focus groups then the mood of some of the staff quickly altered. As Jackson (1993) quite rightly asserts, qualitative research is primarily 'conclusion-orientated' rather than 'decision-orientated' and, as such, my presentation of the data was offered with no expectation of directly improving practice or provision. Yet, it was not long before the validity of the interview data was challenged and then most emphatically and from an unexpected source; namely a group of relatively young GNVQ lecturers, including one who had earlier in the fieldwork period talked to me about her MA research project on educational computing and desire to expand this work into a PhD. As the following excerpt from my field notes illustrates, for this particular member of staff, the interview data were not something that could be engaged with:

NS: As you can see from these quotes, some of the students obviously felt
        this [lack of   contact with ICT] was in some way linked to their gender
        ...
pause for all to begin to read quote
T1:   I don't believe you
pause
NS: ... in what way?
T1:   Gender's got nothing to do with it. I teach all day long and there's never
        any problem with the girls using ICT. You didn't watch any of my
        lessons so how do you know that?
NS: I'm not saying that this is generalisable across *all* classes ... so, how
        would you explain what these two students are referring to?
T1:   They're just making it up or over-exaggerating. It's nothing to do with
        IT
[Research Diary November 1997]

This incident certainly coloured the rest of the evening and again raised yet again the perennial problem of 'whose side' the educational researcher is 'on' (Becker, 1967). Throughout the research I had been at pains not to present myself as any sort of 'ICT expert' but as a researcher who was interested in how students use computers - hoping to be seen in Hammersley and Atkinson's (1995) role of 'acceptable incompetent'. Indeed, for most of the research project I had successfully achieved this. Yet in relaying my findings back to the ICT staff I was thrust into the role of 'unacceptable incompetent' masquerading as 'expert' which was this particular teacher's first line of rebuttal against my data.

A fundamental clash between ICT research and ICT practice is, unfortunately, well-established within the teaching profession. As Clark and Estes (1998, p.5) reflect, there are an:

increasing number of [ICT] colleagues who not only ignore the lack
evidence to support technology enthusiasm but simply do not trust r
Much of this distrust comes from a lack of support one finds in the res
people's intuition about the benefits of educational technology. Their re   ing
seems to suggest that if research does not find evidence for something that
seems so powerful, then research as an inquiry strategy *must* be flawed.

However the incredulity and totality of this particular teacher's denial of
the data also suggests that it was not just my dubious status that they
resented but the inference from the quotes that gender was in fact an issue
in ICT use. That the teacher concerned then went on to question the
plausibility of the students' opinions itself reflects an unwillingness,
perhaps inability, to consider alternative perspectives outside of their own
ICT orthodoxy.

Discussion

As Hammersley and Atkinson (1995, p.285) contend, although reflexivity is
a vital part of qualitative research in the social sciences it is important to
retain a sense of limitation:

> Some discussions of the ethics of social research seem to be premised on the
> idea that social researchers can and should act in an ethically superior manner
> to ordinary people, that they have, or should have, a heightened ethical
> sensibility and responsibility. There is also a tendency to dramatise matters
> excessively, implying a level of likely harm or moral transgression that is far in
> excess of what is typically involved.

Thus it must be borne in mind that discussing the ethics of social research is
often little more than discussing the ethics of day-to-day life. All the
teachers, ICT co-ordinators and senior managers had jobs to do, external
market-driven pressures to respond to and understandably saw me as a
legitimate means of helping them do just that. As I have already hinted, this
had become quickly apparent at the beginning of the fieldwork period.

In retrospect, it should come as no surprise that the introduction of
market forces and open competition into the post-16 sector have increased
the symbolic importance of ICT to 16-19 institutions. Kenway (1995, p.52)
highlights the growing trend of using technology to market education; after
all the idea of 'high-tech sells schools [and] attracts customers'. Thus

institutions are increasingly feeling the pressure to be seen as 'high-tech' from a variety of sources, particularly from potential students fresh from experiencing a computer enriched National Curriculum education. As Kingston et al. (1992, p.10) continue,

> more and more students will present themselves at colleges at 16-plus having had considerable experience of ICT ... With the increasing emphasis on the 'customer' ... colleges must ensure that both the systems and trained staff are in place to cater for a relatively more demanding clientele coming through from schools.

My initial ease of gaining access to schools, colleges and students could be seen as part of institutions' on-going need to be seen and confirmed as being 'high-tech'. As Simons (1995) concedes, in these increasingly market-led times one should expect data and findings to be manipulated and selectively treated by both sponsors and participants. In this way, who was actually in control of the research process was unclear. Having entered an ethically ambiguous pact with the institutions to do what I liked with as many students as possible, did I have the right to then feel concerned when crucial elements of what I had found were ignored, refuted or glossed over because they failed to fit into this underlying celebratory agenda?

In many ways I had expected a degree of selectivity, even incredulity, from practitioners when presented with the research findings - after all, one of the first rules of social science research should be to always bear in mind your unimportance in the relation to what you are researching. However, educationalists have no right to expect students' accounts to correspond with their own notion of what is 'correct' or indeed what is deemed as acceptable in the wider educational technology field. To the contrary, as Bryson and de Castell (1994) argue, there is every need for researchers and teachers to become privy to students' understanding of educational computing in order to make sense of the actual public practices and outcomes which are manifest. To argue, therefore, that the students in my study were 'misconceived' is to negate the entire practice of objective qualitative research and instead attempt to impose a contradictory and dogmatic technicist regime onto an apparently a-technicist set of data. Instead, as Bryson and de Castells (1994, p.216) again point out:

> There is *no* 'master narrative' to be found or made in educational discourses about educational computing. There is no *true story*, no *grand synthesis*. There is instead a *set* of stories, each with its distinctive scope and limits, each of

which imposes, in different ways, a different system of constraints, prescriptives and prohibitions, a different set of limit situations defining the boundaries beyond which teachers and learners cannot go.

ICT may well be permeating society in general, but research consistently has shown that it has failed over the last two decades to take a similar hold in the classroom (e.g. Pelgrum and Plomp, 1991; Watson et al., 1993; Stevenson, 1997). There is a similarly vast body of research which shows that when ICT is used in schools such use is unequal and the preserve of certain students over others (e.g. Sutton, 1991; Schofield, 1995; Singh, 1993). Both these observations were well documented by my own research so, in a sense, I was saying nothing radically new - yet still encountered a 'closed' negative reaction.

As ICT becomes more ingrained into educational settings so too will more researchers from a variety of disciplinary backgrounds be attracted to study it. Hopefully this will go some way to further breaking down the present technicist stranglehold. In the meantime those of us already involved with educational computing would do well to heed Bryson and de Castells' (1994, p.217) conclusion:

> The most important job for researchers concerned to understand the scope and limits of the educational uses of technology is to seek out those stories that are not being circulated, to stop *making sense*, to look for educational technology's version of Foucault's *subjugated knowledges* within which the complications, contradictions and complexities of this new educational domain are most likely and most productively to be discerned. For it will most likely be in the *these* tales, we suspect, that radically innovative possibilities for the transformation of hegemonic practices might best be found.

References

Becker, H. (1967) 'Whose Side Are We On?' *Social Problems*, 14, 3, pp. 329-347.

Beynon, J. and Mackay, H. (1989) 'Information Technology into Education: Towards a Critical Perspective' *Journal of Education Policy* 4, 3, pp.245-257.

Bromley, H. (1997) 'The Social Chicken and the Technological Egg: Educational Computing and the Technology/Society Divide' *Educational Theory*, 47, 1, pp.51-65.

Bryson, M. and de Castell, S. (1994) 'Telling Tales Out of School: Modernist, Critical and Post-modern "True Stories" about Educational Computing' *Journal of Educational Computing Research*, 10, 3, pp. 199-221.

Burgess, R.G. (1983) *'Experiencing Comprehensive Education: a study of Bishop McGregor School'* London: Methuen.

Burgess, R.G. (1985) *'Strategies of Educational Research'* Lewes: Falmer.

Clark, R.E. and Estes, F. (1998) 'Technology or Craft: What are we Doing?' *Educational Technology*, 38, 5, pp.5-11.

Cuban, L. (1986) *'Teachers and Machines: The Classroom Use of Technology Since 1920'* New York: Teachers College Press.

Finch, J. (1985) 'Social Policy and Evaluation: Problems and Possibilities of Using Qualitative Research' in R.G. Burgess, (Ed) *'Issues in Educational Research: Qualitative Methods'* Lewes: Falmer.

Hammersley, M. and Atkinson, P. (1995) *'Ethnography: Principles in Practice'* (Second Edition) London: Routledge.

Hodkinson, P. and Sparkes, A.C. (1993) 'To Tell or Not to Tell? Reflecting on Ethical Dilemmas in Stakeholder Research' *Evaluation and Research in Education*, 7, 3, pp.117-132.

Jackson, P.W. (1993) 'Qualitative Research and its Public' *Qualitative Studies in Education*, 6, 3, pp.227-231

Kenway, J. (1995) 'Reality Bytes: Education, Markets and the Information Superhighway' *Australian Educational Researcher,* 22, 1, 35-65.

Kenway, J. (1996) 'The Information Superhighway and Post-Modernity: the Social Promise and the Social Price' *Comparative Education,* 32, 2, 217-231.

Kingston, P., Morgan, J. and Wagstaff, A. (1992) 'The Impact of New Learning Technologies in Education' *Education and Training*, 34, 5, pp.7-11.

Kitchin, R. (1998) *'Cyberspace: the World in the Wires'* Chichester: Wiley.

Kling, R. (1996) 'The Seductive Equation of Technological Progress with Social Progress' in R. Kling, (Ed) *'Computerisation and Controversy: Value Conflicts and Social Choices'* [Second Edition] San Diego: Academic Press.

Marx, L. (1987) 'Does Improved Technology Mean Progress?' *Technological Review*, 71, pp.33-41.

Papert, S. (1980) *'Mindstorms: Children, Computers and Powerful Ideas'* New York: Harvester Press.

Papert, S. (1995) *'Technology in Schools: Local Fix or Global Transformation'* Remarks to House of Representatives Panel on Technology and Education - October 12th 1995 http://kids.www.media.mit.edu/project/kids/sp-talk.html.

Pelgrum, W. and Plomp, T. (1991) *'The Use of Computers in Education Worldwide: Results from the IEA 'Computers in Education' Survey in 19 Education Systems'* Oxford: Pergamon.

Phtiaka, H. (1994) 'What's In It for Us?' *Qualitative Studies in Education*, 7, 2, pp.155-164.

Qvortrup, L. (1984) *'The Social Significance of Telematics: an Essay on the Information Society'* [Philip Edmonds, trans.] Philadelphia, John Benjamins.

Riddell, S. (1989) 'Exploiting the Exploited? The ethics of feminist research' in R.G. Burgess, (Ed) *'The Ethics of Educational Research'* Lewes: Falmer.

Robins, K. and Webster, F. (1989) *'The Technical Fix: Education, Computers and Industry'* London: Macmillan.

Schofield, J.W. (1995) *'Computers and Classroom Culture'* Cambridge: Cambridge University Press.

Simons, H. (1987) *'Getting to Know Schools in a Democracy: the Politics and Process of Evaluation'* Lewes: Falmer.

Simons, H. (1995) 'The Politics and Ethics of Educational Research in England: contemporary issues' *British Educational Research Journal*, 21, 4, pp.435-449.

Simons, H. (1989) 'Ethics of Case Study in Education Research and Evaluation' in R.G. Burgess, (Ed) *'The Ethics of Educational Research'* Lewes, Falmer.

Singh, P. (1993) 'Institutional Discourse and Practice. A Case Study of the Social Construction of Technological Competence in the Primary Classroom' *British Journal of Sociology of Education*, 14, 1, pp.39-58.

Stevenson Committee (1997) *'Independent Commission into Information and Communications Technology in Secondary Schools 1996/1997'*.

Stonier, T. and Conlin, C. (1985) *'The Three C's: Children, Computers and Communication'* London: Wiley.

Suppes, P. (1966) 'The Uses of Computers in Education' *Scientific American*, 215, pp.207-220.

Sutton, R.E. (1991) 'Equity and Computers in the Schools: A Decade of Research' *Review of Educational Research*, 61, 4, pp.475-503.

Winner, L. (1993) 'Citizen Virtues in a Technological Order' *Inquiry*, 35, pp.341-361.

Woolgar, S. (1990) 'Time and Documents in Researcher Interaction: Some Ways of Making Out What is Happening in Experimental Science' in S. Woolgar, and M. Lynch, (Eds.) *'Representation in Scientific Practice'* Mass: MIT Press.

Young, F.M.D. (1984) 'Information Technology and the Sociology of Education: Some Preliminary Thoughts' *British Journal of Sociology of Education*, 5, 2, pp.205-210.

5 Sex in the field: intimacy and intimidation

AMANDA COFFEY

Introduction

Associating sexual activity and ethnographic fieldwork is nothing new. Indeed the sex lives and sexual relations of *others* have been a long standing concern of social anthropology. For example, both Malinowski (1987) [1929] and Mead (1949) [1928] focused on the sexual lives of 'primitive' societies. Yet despite this fascination and documentation of the 'sexual', anthropologists (and other fieldworkers) have been relatively silent about their own sexuality and sexual experiences. This chapter particularly focuses on aspects of sexual activity, experiences and desires in ethnographic fieldwork. My aim is to explore how 'sex in the field' can aid the quest for a better understanding of the emotional and personal dimensions of fieldwork.

It is not my intention to advocate or encourage those engaged in fieldwork to necessarily seek sexual liaisons with informants or fellow researchers. On the contrary, there are issues of ethics, safety and power that may well work to encourage quite the opposite. Nor is it my aim to criticise, moralise or cast judgement on those fieldworkers who do report sexual encounters during fieldwork. Indeed from a perspective of fieldwork peopled by physical, embodied and emotional social actors, it would be hypocritical to cast the researcher as asexual, or devoid of desire. My concern is however with the ways in which sexual activity, desire and expectation impact upon the lived reality of fieldwork. I contend that the questions and issues raised by focusing on the 'sexual perspective' both illustrate and exaggerate a number of features of fieldwork research. For example, the characteristics of the fieldworker (age, gender, race, sexuality); the relational nature of the research process (establishing and negotiating field roles, relationships, boundaries); and the possible emotions of fieldwork (love, hate, excitement, risk, power, belonging, alienation) can all be analysed through such a focus. The very fact that sexual status and sexual encounters *are* issues for discussion tells us something of the personal and physical intensity which fieldwork involves. That sexual intercourse is a *possibility* and a *reality* (see Kulick and Willson, 1995) demonstrates how intellectual curiosity, physical desire and emotional investment can be construed and experienced in combination. This takes us beyond a consideration of the actual, physical, sexual act toward a much broader set of experiences, constructions and emotions.

Sex(y) settings

The relationship between the personal and the ethnographic is exaggerated in those settings where sex forms part of the explicit research agenda or context. There are some sites of fieldwork where sexuality and sexual status are part of the everyday talk and activity. This sexual dimension of the social setting can have implications for the conduct of fieldwork and the sexual engagement of the researcher. The lives of sex workers (Barnard and McKeganey, 1995), brothel madams (Heyl, 1979), and the sex scene of Times Square (Karp, 1980) are all undeniably concerned with sexual activity of one sort or another. As sex settings they structure the context of fieldwork. Everyday activities and conversations will include sex. Sex will be part of the vocabularies and routines of the setting and the fieldwork. There are other settings where this might well be the case, even though the setting is not explicitly a sexual one. In such settings the sexual dimension may still inform and contextualize the data and the personal fieldwork experience.

There are practical, ethical and personal aspects to fieldwork in sex settings. As Bolton (1996) notes, actual sexual behaviour is not easily observed. How the research is conducted and how data are collected are questions which are particularly relevant. Sexual settings can crystallise the issue of personal involvement or non-involvement for the researcher. Involvement and observation may also have ethical as well as methodological problems attached. Bolton's study of the Belgian gay community (Bolton, 1996) confronts these issues. He participated as a sexually active social actor during his fieldwork. For him it was a natural and inevitable part of both his research and personal experience. Bolton argues that his active, sexual participation was a valuable means of gaining information and insight into the Belgian gay community. Indeed the sorts of data he was able to collect were only possible because of such participation.

> Information obtained post-coitally, (except in quick sex encounters in public places), when people tend to relax and open up about their lives, was always richer, more from the heart and more revealing than the data gathered in a more detached manner. Once one had shared physical and emotional intimacy, sharing other knowledge about oneself seems easier.
> (Bolton, 1996:148-149)

Bolton argues that it would have been extremely difficult for a gay man to investigate such a highly charged erotic environment such as gay sauna baths (where he conducted fieldwork) and not be tempted to participate. He had sexual, intimate and emotional desires which could not easily be divorced from his researcher role. Nor did Bolton advocate that they should be. 'Hanging about' gay venues, bars, baths, and steam rooms was part of his fieldwork and became part of his private life. Engaging in sexual activity was by choice - personally and professionally. Bolton is careful to report that he never engaged in sex purely for the purpose of collecting data; that he never participated in unprotected sex *and* that he was always interested in sexual partners as people *not* simply as convenient informants. The sexual life and activities he participated in were not that different from what he would have done 'back home'. To have not engaged in them would have been to have denied his own sexuality. Although Bolton emphasises his choice and his ethical standpoint he freely admits that in a culture where sexuality, and shared sexual experiences are paramount, it would have been difficult to have fully engaged with the everyday experiences without participating sexually.

It is not necessary to sexually participate in such settings in order to undertake fieldwork, as Humphreys (1970) demonstrated. Humphreys did not engage in sexual activity, although his research setting was explicitly sexual - he was studying gay male sexual encounters in public lavatories ('tea-rooms'). His participation was limited to that of a lookout or 'watchqueen'. By participating in this way Humphreys was able to observe homosexual activity that took place in the tea-rooms, something he would have found much more difficult without some form of participation. It also meant he was in a much better position to engage the participants in meaningful discussion about their activities. Humphreys adopted a quasi-sexual role in the field in order to facilitate his data collection. He was a sexual player, even though he was not a participant in the sexual activity *per se*. *Tearoom trade* has been the subject of some criticism. This has mainly focused on the ways in which Humphreys chose to follow up male customers who frequented the tea-rooms (see Humphreys, 1975 for a methodological and ethical discussion of this). This setting and Humphreys participation highlights the practical and ethical dilemmas of conducting fieldwork in explicitly sexual environments. These are complicated further if we consider gender. For women to participate in 'sexual' fieldwork is perhaps less easy - not least because of the complex juxtaposition of safety and reputation. This should not be taken to imply that physical and sexual safety are not concerns for both men and women. Although it is more usual to associate these concerns with women fieldworkers. Sexual reputation is also a gendered concept, with gender specific routes (sexual prowess versus sexual purity). Bearing this in mind, some women have found a level of participation to be both possible and fruitful. For example, Allison (1994) participated in the everyday life of the Tokyo hostess club. She worked as a hostess in an environment where sex talk was a norm and sexual activity implicit. Allison was part of the sex talk and the sexualizing practices of the club - as both a subject of male desire and as an interactional player. She did not however engage in any sex acts, nor did she observe sexual activity. Her level of participation and the social setting was sexualised but not explicitly sexual.

There is little doubt that participation (more or less) in 'sex' scenes during fieldwork can lead to fruitful data. More doors are open, more conversations possible and meaningful; more everyday practices and routines explicit. The personal dimensions of the experience can also be self-illuminating, in just the same way that any sexual encounter (positive or negative, scheduled or not) can be. The collection of 'sexy' data, and the possibility for a personal sexual experience are two outcomes of fieldwork in sexual settings. Such fieldwork also illustrates and exaggerates the issues of boundary and positionality in research. The cultural importance and centrality of sex may make it potentially more difficult to establish and recognise the boundaries between the personal and the professional, the fieldworker and the self. Even where participation is limited, the sexualizing of the self becomes a crucial part of the fieldwork experience. In these instances, sexuality, privacy and data collection are interwoven. The cultural importance of sex in these settings makes the positionality of the sexual self more transparent and real, yet more difficult to separate from the fieldworker self. Explicitly sexual settings make it possible to acknowledge the ways in which fieldwork can be sexual and embodied. They can provide a sexual vocabulary and a context within which to test and explore the rules of behaviour and action.

Settings do not need to be conceived explicitly and centrally as sexual to be sexually charged - for researcher and researched. For example, the nude beach is not necessarily a sexual scene - yet the association between nudity, sex and beach life makes it so. Douglas et al (1977) observed very little in the way of public and explicit sexual acts. But there were stories and accounts of sexual intercourse, sexual activities and sexual violence happening on the beach. Indeed while sexual activity was not part of the nude beach in any explicit sense, sex was part of the everyday world the researchers observed and heard. As participant observers, Douglas and his colleagues contributed to and participated in this social world.

> An important part of this 'going natural' was learning the body code and the situated body language of the nude beach. The situated language, the subcultural dialect of a universal body-code, is being created slowly to deal with the scene as people come increasingly to grasp and understand it. Much of the communication on the beach, especially the most important kinds about sex, is done entirely in terms of the body-code - facial expressions, the way one walks, autonomic responses (from erections to quavering voices).
> (Douglas, 1977)

Douglas and his colleagues immersed themselves in the 'sex' scene of the nude beach. The beach was 'told' as a place for sexual display, finding partners, dealing with hang-ups and frigidity, voyeurism and gay cruising. All of these activities were ongoing and contributed to the nude beach as a site of sexual narrative and sexual activity. Sex was part of the vocabulary, rituals, interactions and everyday activities of the beach. Hence it was a central part of the ethnographic analysis of understanding the social world of the nude beach. Sex was ethnographically and analytically significant. Parry's (1982) research in a British naturist club is less explicit about the ways in which sex is implicated in an everyday context. Unlike the nude beach, the naturist club was mainly a social location for married couples (indeed there were strict restrictions on membership by single, unattached males and females), yet Parry notes issues around sexuality and sexual display. The naturist club had strict rules around certain aspects of sex-related behaviour. Naturism (nudity in a particular social context) was explicitly presented as non-sexual. Physical and overtly sexual contact was, in fact, less acceptable in the club than in many other social settings. The demonstrative actions of fondling, hugging and kissing were usually viewed as inappropriate and certainly not encouraged as a norm. While nudity was explicit, physical displays such as penile erection were denied as sexual. Parry was an unusual member of the club, being a single woman who joined on her own (she did not conduct covert research, but access to undertake the study depended upon her becoming a member). While the club were aware of her researcher status, a condition of her attendance was adherence of the club rules - including nudity and attention to the 'sexual' rules of the club. Her observations suggest a conscious attempt by the club to desexualize a potentially sexually charged environment.

In just the same way as explicitly sexual settings, examples like the nude beach and the naturist club present the fieldworker with rules, boundaries, and vocabulary about sexual behaviour, display and appropriateness. Sometimes these rules and boundaries are implicit - the nude beach did not have explicit rules about sex, yet what was appropriate, acceptable, desirable or lewd was discernible. Very public, very overt sexual activity was 'not permitted'. The Naturist club had much more explicit and understood rules about sexual action and behaviour. Many of Parry's informants were reluctant to discuss matters of a sexual nature. They were seemingly unwilling to sexualize their club participation and activities, and certainly did not wish to give Parry any reason to do so. Yet in divorcing nudity from sex, the club and its participants were engaging in a sexual dialogue with each other and with the researcher, albeit unspoken and muted. This de-sexualising of the naturist club reflects a particular aspect of fieldwork and ethnographic writing. Ethnography, to some extent, trades on ironic contrasts with regard to sex and sexuality. Both intrinsically and contemporarily the fieldworker has often been keen to 'look beyond' the sexual in explicitly sexual settings. The sexual has often been desexualised - sex has been taken to be indicative of more general social interactions and cultural events. Rituals around sexuality have been analysed in terms of the everyday activities of the fieldsite. Sex in this way has almost been accidental or incidental to the analysis of the social setting. Sex(ual) settings have been reanalysed in terms of their interactional process and personal-structural contexts shifting the focus away from the sexual and the erotic. By contrast settings and organisations not explicitly sexual have been sexualised; that is the *hidden* sexuality of the site has been brought to the fore and used as a tool of analysis. For example contemporary studies of organisational settings have focused on sexuality as an analytical framework. (There is a whole literature on sexuality and organisation, see for example Hearn et al, 1989; Witz, Halford and Savage, 1996).

Intimacy and intimidation

In this section attention is turned toward the more general issues of sex in the field. The actual or perceived sexual status of the researcher has a number of implications - for incorporation into the field, fieldwork relations and relationships, the maintenance of fieldwork boundaries, the reproduction of gender and so on. While the physical acts of sexual intercourse are perhaps implicit here, they are often shrouded in terms of marriage, love, children, *and* for women especially, personal safety and cultural expectations of appropriate behaviour. Such aspects are all, of course, bound up with the expectations and assumptions of a sexual relationship, although the physical act of sex is still a relatively taboo subject for the ethnographic account. However there are a small corpus of authors who have chosen to write about the sex act in fieldwork from a personal, experiential perspective, most notably the contributors to the Kulick and Willson (1995) collection of anthropological fieldwork experiences. The particular nature of anthropological fieldwork may make some anthropologists especially susceptible to the formation of personal (and sexual) relationships in the field. It is documented (and more generally assumed by the anthropological community) that, for social anthropologists, fieldwork is a deeply bounded, prolonged, personal experience. The tradition and expectation of (partial) immersion in the field is still strong (Coffey and Atkinson, 1996). In such contexts it is both understandable, and perhaps unsurprising, that deeply personal relationships are formed. The anthropologist 'lives' the field and is most intimately a part of the place and people that are being studied. While not all social anthropologists 'go away', and there is an increasing amount of anthropological fieldwork being conducted 'at home' (often referred to as indigenous ethnography), the bounded, insular and private conception of the fieldwork experience still holds. 'In the field' and then 'coming back from the field' are still real categories and temporal boundaries.

For others engaged in fieldwork, it is less the case that full immersion and engagement is the norm. For example some sociologists and educationalists have immersed themselves in the field and lived there for an extended period of time. But certainly for many, even while 'doing fieldwork', a separate personal life is maintained - going home in the evenings, keeping regular contact with supervisors, colleagues and departments, maintaining friendships, relationships and social contacts outside of the field. For these researchers, fieldwork is more tightly framed and distinctive from the rest of their lives. While the fieldwork experience can still be a personal experience, the boundaries between fieldwork and a personal perspective are more tightly drawn on a day-to-day basis. That is not to say that such boundaries are not blurred or open to redefinition. Nor should it imply that, unless we completely immerse ourselves in the field for an extended and unbroken period of time, we are immune from the formation of deeply personal *or* meaningful *or* sexual relations. The very nature of fieldwork implies a personal dimension. However, few sociologists, or educationalists for example have written about actual sexual encounters in the field. That *might* be because they are less likely to occur in fieldwork with strong home/work, in the field/out of the field boundaries. When there is a sense of a reality outside of the field, it might be possible to establish and maintain personal and sexual boundaries. This may be less easily achieved where the fieldworker is getting all of their personal and social as well as professional stimulation from the field. Of course it is equally possible that the possibilities of sexual encounters are simply more readily accepted by social anthropologists, and hence more easily confessed. Although as Dubisch (1995) notes, celibacy is considered the norm during anthropological fieldwork, and accounts of exceptions to this are still rare.

It is difficult to analyse fully and understand sexual relations that occur during fieldwork as we do not really know the extent of such relations. There is a strong oral culture within the ethnographic community generally, with tales and anecdotes of sex in the field. While this does not necessarily imply that sexual encounters during fieldwork are particularly common experiences, it does indicate that the possibilities of sexual activity exist. It should be noted here that I am not connecting fieldwork to an inevitable expectation or reality of sexual encounter. Rather, the possibilities and realities can be used reflexively to examine the place of intimacy and the personal in fieldwork. There are a number of different contexts within which sex in the field can occur. It would be nonsense here to try to homogenise a wide and diverse range of experiences and emotions. But the possibility (and actuality) of sexual encounters in the field relates personal intimacy to the fieldwork experience. Where sex does occur, the field is eroticised. In turn this has consequences for the ways in which fieldwork is conducted, data are collected and experiences remembered. For example, there is a tradition of married (or cohabiting) couples going into the field together and jointly participating in fieldwork (see for example Corbin and Corbin, 1984; 1987; Oboler, 1986; Scheper-Hughes, 1992; Schrijvers, 1993; Vera-Sanso, 1993; Wolf, 1992). The marital status and relationship can be an important aspect of the identity work and the establishment of relations in the field. The status of 'couple', and with this the implicit assumptions about sexuality, establishes and maintains a fieldwork boundary. The fieldworker 'couple' come to the field with a distinct, collective identity already in place. While this may be exposed, challenged or modified over the course of fieldwork, nevertheless this sort of (sexual) relationship locates the fieldworker in a social world beyond the field.

These relationships have usually existed prior to fieldwork and are taken to the field intact. There are other examples of romance and marriage which occur during fieldwork. Fieldwork can provide the opportunity for the establishment of intimate, and in some cases, long lasting commitments between the ethnographer and a significant 'other' in the field. Gearing (1995), for instance, fell in love and eventually married her *best informant* [sic] during fieldwork in the West Indies. What began as a productive, professional relationship became a personal and sexual relationship.

> As we spent more time together, discussing our respective family histories, I came to trust him and began to see him as a person I cared for deeply, as well as a person to whom I was strongly sexually attracted. I was also impressed by the sacrifices E.C. made to help me, and his refusal to take any money in return, even though I explained to him how valuable his help was to me. E.C. was always considerate, was concerned about my safety, and often brought me small gifts of food or flowers.
> The combination of personal and professional attractions was incredibly appealing, and actually impossible to resist. My intellectual excitement kept pace with my physical attraction as I learned more and more.
> (Gearing, 1995:199)

For Gearing, her relationship and eventual marriage to 'E.C.' was personally fulfilling *and* fruitful ethnography. Gearing describes her fieldsite as a potentially sexually dangerous setting. Prior to her relationship with EC (the man she marries), she frequently encountered sexual harassment and intimidation. Though she is absolutely clear that fear did not propel her into the relationship (and indeed she still received unwanted sexual advances even after marriage), her marriage did make it safer to visit places, and to collect data that would otherwise have been problematic. EC helped her gain access to men's perceptions of gender and sexuality. Gearing argues that she was also able to gain an 'intimate view of the erotic dimension of Vincentian life' (1995:202). Her sexual relationship in the field became an important aspect of the fieldwork itself. While a rewarding and sexually compatible relationship in itself, her marriage was also central to the construction of her self identity within the field. It provided an opportunity for making sense of the sexual and cultural context in which she was living. There are other examples of romantic encounters in the field. Not all of them last beyond the fieldwork. Blackwood (1995) describes how her lesbian relationship ended on her return to north America. However despite the end of the relationship Blackwood provides an account of it as loving, sexual and meaningful. Moreover it is difficult to separate her fieldwork experience and identity from this personal encounter. The fieldwork, and her retrospective memories of it, are interwoven with/in the relationship.

Long-term (and emotionally committed) relationships are one outcome of sex in the field. Though they are by no means the only or indeed commonest experience of sexual liaisons during fieldwork. As I have noted elsewhere in this chapter sex can be part of the field setting, and entered into as part of the fieldwork (as in the case of Bolton, 1996). Our sexuality, and its expression in the field, is not confined to the negotiation of romantic or permanent intimacy. Sexual encounters do not need to be long-term in order to be identified as epistemologically significant. Dubisch (1995a, 1995b), provides a good example of how her sexual encounters in the field were part of her on-going identity work. During fieldwork trips to Greece Dubisch had sexual relationships with two local men. The sexual encounters were part of a fieldwork process of locating herself within the field. Whether or not one has sex in the field, Dubisch argues that sexuality is an aspect of the self which may be particularly challenged in the field, and her sexual relationships made her more aware of the complexity of identities and relationships that we bring to and take from the field. Wade's account of his lovers in the field further illustrates this point.

> My motives for forming these relationships were not essentially about gaining access to information in a simple sense, but rather about a desire to transcend the separateness that I perceived as distancing me from a constructed otherness of black culture, by participating in a relation classed as the most intimate in my own culture, one not just of sex, but of 'love'.
> (Wade, 1993: 203)

Sexual intimacy is one particular sort of intimacy which can be experienced during fieldwork. It can symbolise one of the most intimate of relationships between researcher and researched (that is not to deny that sexual encounters can be casual, and far from intimate). While most of us do not experience sexual relations during fieldwork, many of us are faced with decisions over the level of intimacy and closeness with our informants and research participants. El-Or (1997) questions the scope for intimacy in fieldwork.

> Intimate relationships between researcher and informants, blur the subject-object connection they actually maintain. Being able to communicate on equal levels of everyday life, sharing feelings and thoughts, revealing anxieties, dreams or desires obscure the working bond they've agreed to preserve. Intimacy thus offers a cosy environment for the ethnographic journey, but at the same time an illusive one.
> (El-Or, 1997:188)

While El-Or is not describing a sexually intimate relationship, her general point about the limitations of intimacy may be equally valid in such cases. El-Or questions the endurance of intimacy and reciprocal relations precisely because at the heart of fieldwork is the quest for information. Sexual relations during fieldwork blur the boundary between subject and object in emotional and physical ways. There is therefore a contradiction in discussing and *confessing* such relations. On the one hand it may be both ethnographically productive and personally important to be reflective about sexual encounters in the field. On the other hand by writing about these intimate relations in the context of fieldwork, the sexual encounter becomes part of the analysis of fieldwork. Knowing and writing about sex in the field simultaneously reveals the intimate possibilities of fieldwork and denies that intimacy as purely personal.

The sexual encounters I have discussed above have been framed in terms of personal gratification and, in some cases, ethnographic payoff. The relationships have been recounted as reciprocal and certainly as ones to which the fieldworker was consenting. In the literature on gender and fieldwork there are also accounts of sexual harassment. These are usually, though not exclusively, told be women (see for example Gurney, 1985; Warren, 1988). Tales of sexual intimidation and harassment have usually been told in terms of sexist language, gender joking, innuendo and inappropriate, unwelcome touching. On a few occasions this intimidation actually results in physical and emotional sexual assault. Moreno (1995) provides an account of sexual intimidation during fieldwork, which resulted in her being sexually and emotionally raped. Her example is highly illustrative of the fragility of field relations, and as such has significance beyond the immediacy of a sexual attack. While clearly distressing, physically and emotionally scarring, the rape was able to highlight, for Moreno, the false dichotomy between professional and private. Moreno (1995:243-244) remembers her feelings immediately following the violation of her sexual self 'overwhelmed by a flood of information on gender relations and sexuality, but I was in no position to record, understand, or utilise the material. I felt naked, a simple civilian, a deserter from the anthropological field'. The violation of her body meant that for a while she was, understandably, unable to analyse the meanings of the encounter. However, on reflection, Moreno was able to use her experience to renegotiate her field identity

> In the field the false division of time and space between the 'professional and the private' that underpins the supposedly gender-neutral identity of the anthropologist collapses completely. In the field it is not possible to maintain the fiction of a genderless self. In the field, one is marked.
> (1995:246-247)

As a sexualised, gendered self, the fieldworker is both open to the pleasure of sexual intimacy and the violence of sexual intimidation. Both are deeply affective at the personal, private level of the individual self.   This positionality of the sexual self within the field is something to which several authors have turned their attention.   In relation to sexuality, and more specifically to sexual encounters a debate ensues over the relationship between the self and sex in the field. Wengle (1988), for example has argued that in order for the anthropological self to remain whole and secure in his [sic] identity, celibacy is crucial. Celibacy in the field forces desire and sexual need to be located outside of the field, at home and thus in a private sphere (and separate from fieldwork). Kulick (1996) among others, has expressed concerns with this line of argument, arguing that the psychological argument put forward by Wengle effectively 'silences' sexual relationships and partners in the field. To deny our sexuality, sexual identity, partners and lovers is, in effect to render ourselves as asexual. It serves to reinforce a false dichotomy between the fieldworker self and other selves. This denies the reality and complexity of fieldwork and the identity work that it entails. The self is positioned in a range of contexts -

cultural, historical, political, gendered and sexual. Desire and sex in the field enables the fieldworker to experience a positionality first hand. Whether the desire originates from them, or whether they are the objects/subjects of that desire, they are able to use their experiences to locate the self and the fieldwork. Sexual encounters can be viewed as personally productive and ethnographically productive. They allow for reflections on the fieldwork, relationships, people, the sexuality of others, the nature of self and the production of knowledge. Most of the authors who have discussed their experiences of desire and sex in the field are all too aware of the ethical issues which this involves. At one level there are lessons that emerge from Said's (1978) critique of sustained *orientalism*. The erotic is quickly associated with the exotic, and in studying 'other' cultures ethnographers have been accused of exploiting and 'otherizing'. This is, of course, part of a more general ethical problem of power and exploitation in fieldwork. Sexual encounters perhaps crystallise these ethical dilemmas - cutting across the personal and the professional, as well as genders, sexualities, cultures, ethnicities, ages. Dubisch (1996) observes that as an intimate encounter, sex is not of itself bad or any worse than other fieldwork activity.

> We do almost everything else with our 'informants': share their lives, eat with them, attend their rituals, become part of their families, even become close friends, and sometimes establish life-long relationships. At the same time, we 'use' them to further our goals, writing and speaking in public contexts about personal and even intimate aspects of their lives, appropriating these lives for our own professional purposes. Could a sexual relationship be any more intimate, committing, or exploitative than our normal relations with the 'natives'? (In some societies, it might even be less so.)
> (Gearing, 1995:31)

Sex is but one aspect of the positionality of the self and the relationships that are formed in the field. Like other aspects it can be revealing and epistemologically valuable (as well as personally rewarding) if it is reflected upon critically and honestly. Gearing (1996) argues for an emotionally aware ethnography - and in doing so she recognises that emotion can include fear, intimidation and hurt as well as desire, attraction, caring and love. The points she makes is that by ignoring our emotions we are denying they exist and hence denying that they do have an impact on the knowledge we produce, and that in itself could be deemed unethical. As she argues

I do not think that effective ethnographic research can be done without emotional engagement, and the pursuit of a methodology that ignores what we learn from our emotions is undermining the validity of the resulting information [...] in fieldwork as in all of life, sensation, emotion and intellect operate simultaneously to structure and interpret our experience of the world.   Our emotional reactions, and those to which we interact, guide our analysis of life 'at home' as well as 'in the field'.
(Gearing 1996:209)

Conclusion

In conclusion I turn to the issue of talking and writing about 'sex in the field'. Should sexual encounters during fieldwork be counted as data and do they have impact on our ability to conduct fieldwork?   Freeman's (1991) attack on Mead because of the affairs 'she might have had' during her fieldwork addresses the second of these points.   Responding to what Landes (1970) describes as gossip about Mead's relationships, Freeman argued that Mead's personal sexuality discredited her ability as an ethnographer (see Bryman, 1994 for a summary of the Mead/Freeman controversy).   While Mead's relationships are largely unsubstantiated, the accounts that I have presented in this chapter suggest this is at best a simplistic view and at worst a gross misunderstanding of the issues. Without wishing to further expand on this debate here, I would suggest that sexual liaisons in the field may blur the boundaries of fieldwork.   There is however little evidence that they unequivocally hinder fieldwork.   On the contrary in some instances they clarify and aid a better understanding of the process.   There are still relatively few 'confessions' which overtly or explicitly refer to sexual encounters or desire in the field.   *Yet* when they do, a lot of what is said does strike home.   We are emotional beings engaged in fieldwork and therefore it is perhaps surprising that there are not more emotional and sexual attachments in the field.   Perhaps there are, perhaps we just do not talk about them.   There is still perhaps the myth of the neutral, semi-detached, 'scientific' and 'objective' ethnographer in operation, in theory if not in practice.   We should certainly not automatically privilege the accounts of ethnographers who 'confess' to sexual relationships in the field.   The epistemological productiveness of such fieldwork relationships is dependent not on the sex act in itself, but in the ways in which erotic subjectivity and experiences of the ethnographer can be harnessed to further understand the field and the self, and the boundaries and connectedness between the two. Accounts of sexuality and desire do have the potential for an exploration of fieldwork relationships, their nature, basis and consequences. Whether we choose to talk and write about desire and sex will always be a matter of individual choice *and* will always, perhaps, be bounded by disciplinary issues of boundary, power, exploitation, distance and engagement. Regardless of whether we choose to talk or 'confess', the sexual self is part of our being and part of the way we experience our lives. Not reflecting upon that, silences the people with whom we forge relationships, engage in sexual encounters with, fall in love with, are sexually intimate with (and indeed intimidated by). Consequently it is both realistic and epistemologically valuable to at least confess and have the conversation with ourselves.

References

Allison, A. (1994) *Nightwork: Sexuality, Pleasure and Corporate Masculinity in a Tokyo Hostess Club.* Chicago: University of Chicago Press.

Barnard, M. and McKeganey, N. (1995) *Sex Work on the Streets: Prostitutes and their Clients.* Buckingham: Open University Press.

Bolton, R. (1996) 'Tricks, friends and lovers: erotic encounters in the field' in D. Kulick and M. Willson (eds.) *Taboo: Sex, Identity and Erotic Subjectivity in Anthropological Fieldwork.* London and New York: Routledge. pp.140-167.

Blackwood, E. (1995) 'Falling in love with another lesbian: reflections on identity in fieldwork', in D. Kulick and M. Willson (eds.) *Taboo: Sex, Identity and Erotic Subjectivity in Anthropological Fieldwork.* London and New York: Routledge. pp.51-75.

Bryman, A. (1994) 'The Mead/Freeman controversy: some implications for qualitative researchers', in R.G. Burgess (ed.) *Studies in Qualitative Methodology 4: Issues in qualitative research.* London: JAI Press.

Coffey, A. and Atkinson, P. (1996) *Making Sense of Qualitative Data: Complementary Research Strategies.* Thousand Oaks CA.: Sage.

Corbin, J.R. and Corbin, M.P. (1984) *Compromising Relations: Kith, Kin and Class in Andalusia.* Aldershot: Gower.

Corbin, J.R. and Corbin, M.P. (1987) *Urbane Thought: Culture and Class in an Andalusian City.* Aldershot: Avebury.

Douglas, J.D., Rasmussen, P.K. and Flanagan, C.A. (1977) *The Nude Beach.* Beverley Hills, CA: Sage.

Dubisch, J. (1995a) 'Lovers in the field; sex, dominance, and the female anthropologist', in D. Kulick and M. Willson (eds.) *Taboo: Sex, Identity and Erotic Subjectivity in Anthropological Fieldwork.* London and New York: Routledge. pp.29-50.

Dubisch, J. (1995b) *In a Different Place: Pilgrimage, Gender and Politics at a Greek Island Shrine.* Princeton, NJ: Princeton University Press.

El-Or, T. (1997) 'Do you really know how they make love? The limits on intimacy with ethnographic informants', in R. Hertz (ed.), *Reflexivity and Voice.* Thousand Oaks, CA: Sage. pp.169-189.

Freeman, D. (1991) 'There's tricks i' th' world: an historical analysis of the Samoan researches of Margaret Mead', *Visual Anthropology Review*, 7 (1): 103-128.

Gearing, J. (1995) ' Fear and loving in the West Indies: research from the heart (as well as the head)' in D. Kulick and M. Willson (eds.) *Taboo: Sex, Identity and Erotic Subjectivity in Anthropological Fieldwork.* London and New York: Routledge. pp.186-218.

Gurney, J.N. (1985) 'Not one of the guys: the female researcher in a male-dominated setting' *Qualtitative Sociology*, 8: 42-62

Hearn, J., Sheppard, D.L., Tancred-Sheriff, P. and Burrell, G. (eds.) (1989) *The Sexuality of Organization.* London: Sage.

Heyl, B. (1979) *The Madam as Entrepeneur: Career Management in House Prostitution.* New Brunswick, NJ: Transaction Books.

Humphreys, L. (1970) *Tearoom Trade: a Study of Homosexual Encounters in Public Places.* Chicago: Aldine.

Humphreys, L. (1975) *Tearoom Trade: Impersonal Sex in Public Places.* (Enlarged edition with a retrospective on ethical issues). New York: Aldine de Gruyter.

Karp, D.A. (1980) 'Observing behaviour in public places: problems and strategies', in W.B. Shaffir, R.A. Stebbins and A. Turowetz (eds), *Fieldwork Experience: Qualitative approaches to social research.* New York: St Martin's Press.

Kulick, D. (1996) 'The sexual life of anthropologists: erotic subjectivity and ethnographic work', in D. Kulick and M. Willson (eds.) *Taboo: Sex, Identity and Erotic Subjectivity in Anthropological Fieldwork.* London and New York: Routledge. pp.1-28.

Kulick, D. and Willson, M. (eds.) (1995) *Taboo: Sex, Identity and Erotic Subjectivity in Anthropological Fieldwork.* London and New York: Routledge.

Landes, R. (1970) 'A woman anthropologist in Brazil', in P. Golde (ed.), *Women in the Field: Anthropological Experiences.* Berkeley, CA: University of California Press.

Malinowski, B. (1987) [1929] *The Sexual Life of Savages.* Boston, Mass: Beacon Press.

Mead, M. (1949) [1928] *Coming of Age in Samoa: A Psychological Study of Primitive Youth for Western Civilization.* New York: Mentor Books.

Moreno, E. (1995) 'Rape in the field: reflections from a survivor', D. Kulick and M. Willson (eds.) *Taboo: Sex, Identity and Erotic Subjectivity in Anthropological Fieldwork.* London and New York: Routledge. pp.219-250.

Oboler, R.S. (1986) 'For better or worse: anthropologists and husbands in the field', in T.L. Whitehead and M.E. Conaway (eds.) *Self, Sex and Gender in Cross-Cultural Fieldwork.* Urbana, ILL: University of Illinois Press.

Parry, O. (1982) 'Campaign for respectability: a study of organised British naturism'. MSc. Econ. Dissertation, University College, Cardiff.

Parry, O. (1987) 'Uncovering the ethnographer', in N. McKeganey and S. Cunningham-Burley (eds.) *Enter the sociologist: reflections on the practice of sociology.* Aldershot: Avebury. pp.82-96.

Said, E. (1978) *Orientalism.* London: Routledge and Kegan Paul.

Scheper-Hughes, N. (1992) *Death Without Weeping: the Violence of Everyday Life in Brazil.* California: University of California Press.

Schrijvers, J. (1983) 'Manipulated motherhood: the marginalization of peasant women in the North-Central province of Sri Lanka', *Development and Change,* 14 (2): 185-211.

Schrijvers, J. (1993) 'Motherhood experienced and conceptualized: changing images in Sri Lanka and the Netherlands' in D. Bell, P. Caplan and W.J. Karim (eds.), *Gendered Fields: Women, Men and Ethnography.* London: Routledge. pp.143-158.

Vera-Sanso, P. (1993) 'Perception, east and west: a Madras encounter,' in D. Bell, P. Caplan and W.J. Karim (eds.), *Gendered Fields: Women, Men and Ethnography.* London: Routledge. pp.159-167.

Wade, P. (1993) 'Sexuality and masculinity in fieldwork amoung Columbian Blacks' in D. Bell, P. Caplan and W.J. Karim (eds.),

Gendered Fields: Women, Men and Ethnography. London: Routledge. pp.199-214.

Warren, C.A.B. (1988) *Gender Issues in Field Research*. Newbury Park CA.: Sage.

Wengle, J. (1988) *Ethnographers in the Field: The Psychology of Research*. Tuscaloosa, Ala.: University of Alabama Press.

Witz, A.; Halford, S. and Savage, M. (1996) 'Organized bodies: gender, sexuality and embodiment in contemporary organizations', in A. Adkins and V. Merchant, *Sexualizing the Social*. London: Macmillan. pp.173-190.

Wolf, M. (1992) *A Thrice Told Tale: Feminism, postmodernism and ethnographic responsibility*. Stanford CA.: Stanford University Press.

6 Roles and responsibilities in researching poor women in Brazil

BANI DEV MAKKAR

To say that a slave society cannot adopt liberal ideas is to forget that ideologies marry without asking sociologists for permission.
(DaMatta, 1995, p.278).

Introduction

Apart from the obvious difficulty with distance, many obstacles arise from researching projects overseas, which the researcher is rarely prepared for. Studying to do research is never the same as actually doing it and although preparation is vital, it can never be adequate for the unpredictable, spontaneous events that mark research in the field as a unique experience. Our ethical and moral codes are too often challenged by the unexpected. We are placed in situations so specific, and sometimes so unforeseen that it is often our judgement that becomes the most ready tool at such moments. This is not to say that the outcomes of these decisions are necessarily precarious, but that simply 'hands-on' research is really about the unknown. How our judgements are informed will therefore seriously effect how we set out to investigate the research setting and ultimately how we view the results.

This chapter focuses upon the dilemmas that arise in the overseas context, and although some of them may be familiar territory, many of them are extenuated by the context or made more blatant, or indeed have particular consequences and meanings to those involved because of the geographical divides and sometimes ideological separation of ideas.

Ideological categories

Much is talked about covert/overt research means and ends, informed consent and the right to privacy (Bulmer, 1982; Kimmel 1988) and less about the more subtle aspects of research ethics. In comparative research, the dominant cultural forms, that is, the paradigms in which we are working, are rarely seen as an ethical point of consideration. In this chapter, I shall argue that the cultural 'bubbles' that we work within require guidance and regulation in the same way that other research practices are monitored, if we are to avoid an ethnocentric evaluation of cultures and societies.

On embarking on the research topic we are faced with many decisions. It is important to be aware of how research questions are being constructed and what is informing the enquiry that lies behind them. As the trajectory of the project progresses, interactions with people and organisations, and within situations and contexts get underway. Of course they emerge in a particular way according to how they are being researched, but as well, we as researchers are also emerging in some sense. The importance of the project to us can override the perspectives others have who are also involved or who become involved. This is not to advocate the abandonment of the research project if and when it reaches a stage when the researcher finds that her efforts would be better spent adopting the objectives of those 'being' researched. Rather, there is a need to put the researcher and project in proper context and part of the bigger picture.

Conventionally research has been taught on the basis of detachment and impartiality. More recently this has been reassessed and the relationship between researcher and researched has been questioned. The most visible of these challenges has come from feminist researchers. Anne Oakley is one of the most well-known proponents of an alternative approach to interviewing (Oakley, 1981). Many approaches adopted by feminists in their research projects have either sought to create a different method or indeed used a feminist perspective to inform the way in which the research is approached. Reinharz's anthology of *Feminist Methods in Social Research* (Reinharz, 1992), has sought to highlight the many methods used by feminist researchers, and incorporates various techniques from feminist interview research, to what has been called 'original feminist research methods'. A link between these approaches can perhaps be seen in the way power is re-visited in relation to the researcher/research participant encounter. The tacit assumption that in some sense the researcher wholly defines the research because it is (s)he, who instigates it, is put into question.

> The question of difference is one with the question of identity. It is becoming the critical question for feminist theorising in all the disciplines including social science research methods as feminists begin to question and challenge the implicit male perspective of the dominant paradigms, methodological strictures, and theoretical assumptions of the various disciplines.
> (Reinharz, 1992, p.3)

Social relations can indeed be expanded beyond the researcher/researched dichotomy to broader areas of social life. Social power is manifested in many and various forms, amongst groups and individuals, institutions and ideas. Thus the ways in which we view the research setting and the people within it is highly subject to our own social position. The influence of ideas that we therefore construct and disseminate are not devoid of our social location. Tim May views this problem in the following way;

> Social power is not evenly distributed between groups. The definition that there exists a problem will often depend on the relative power that the people who define the social problem have over those who are defined: for instance, those with access to the media possess more power in the construction of social problems than those with limited access. Given these factors rather than simply accepting the definition, it is equally valid to examine the process through which a phenomenon became defined as a problem. In this way the accepted truth that there exists a problem is abandoned in favour of researching how it became constructed as one.
> (May, 1996, p.36)

Constant vigilance over our need to label a problem in an attempt to justify our research endeavours and to give us something to find an answer to is a necessity. Continual questioning of the values we have is vital despite the difficulties in accounting for their worth afforded by the wider society, which may influence the research (May, 1996, p.37). Commenting on much of the research that has been carried out on Brazil, Roberto A. DaMatta (1995) remarks that what has been used is 'an individualised epistemology to study a reality that functions relationally' (DaMatta, 1995, p.281). He goes on to say, in his discussion of how Brazil has been traditionally researched from the outside, that everything becomes exaggerated until 'we end up more interested in listing theoretically implausible amalgams than exploring their deeper logic' (DaMatta, 1995, p.270).

The legacy of Western (frequently male) *explorer* in which a heroic individual goes out into the 'unknown' and makes a discovery, and offers this information to the world has perhaps had its day. Or has it? It may be that it has transformed its cloak and in fact endures in different guises, one of which is the modern day 'researcher explorer'. The information collected is taken *back* to enrich *our* understanding of *other* cultures and of our own. The idea that places and peoples may be *discovered* can also be advanced to the discovery of social and historical relations and practices. We have a certain responsibility to acknowledge our place within the context, in conjunction with those who have a cultural and emotional knowledge of the social setting. This can be applied to all social research, especially that which seeks to evaluate potentially vulnerable elements of society, whether this be an individual, community, research population or ideology (as in a post-colonial hegemony of one paradigm over another). DaMatta comments that observers of Latin America:

> Rarely question their own starting point. They assume their position to be logical and precise to the extent that they are part of a system capable of defining itself with a word (capitalism, modernity, progress), two or three well-known concepts (usually made up by the observers, and on their own terms), and only one sort of logic - the excluded middle (the *tertium non datur* of the ancient philosophers) - that does not allow apples and oranges to mix. (DaMatta, 1995).

Thus the task of stepping out of our familiar concepts that form our tools of analysis of how societies are organised is quite a challenging one. Nevertheless it is an important one if we are to successfully analyse, understand and represent cultures that are not our own.

Women as a category of analysis

The creation of a *single* 'third world woman' who can be seen as being portrayed as 'oppressed', 'defenceless', 'passive', 'powerless' and 'dependent' has become one such category of analysis. The problem with this is primarily that *all* women from this sphere are assigned such attributes and thus the relations between them and men are completely confined within the parameters of gender roles which take no account of the ethnic or class context. Thus as Mohanty articulates it;

> Because women are thus constituted as a coherent group, sexual difference becomes coterminous with female subordination, and power is automatically defined in binary terms: people who have it (read: men), and people who do not (read: women).
> (Mohanty, 1991:64)

Mohanty posits a view of colonisation as being chiefly discursive. This, she says is based upon a particular use and categorisation in learning and science of women in the developing world, that adopts specific categories which are perceived prior to any analysis.

The 'sexual division of labour' and 'women' are not equal categories of analysis. Such concepts need to be looked at in their specific context for them to be meaningful. To see these concepts as though they are universal categories is a mistake, since this can lead to the idea that there is a unity in 'oppression, interests, and struggles' between the two genders (Mohanty, 1991).

Thus, in taking an example of Indian women of different castes and classes, who may have a commonality against police mistreatment, it is also the brutality of the police that needs to be seen in context, and within its social setting. Thus we may question and analyse the social and political context which has given rise to violence by state forces.

> Strategic coalitions which construct oppositional political identities for themselves are based on generalization and provisional unities, but the analysis of these group identities cannot be based on universalistic, ahistorical categories.
> (Mohanty, 1991:69)

In response to those who argue that this may simply result in cultural relativism, the counter-response is that categories that supposedly 'transcend' gender, class and race are in danger of advancing an ethnocentric viewpoint. It is thus as important to look at the context in conjunction with the women that are being studied as it is to look at the situation of the women themselves. The issue of the veil, perhaps one of the most controversial examples of debate amongst feminists and cultural theorists, is one that, although screams of the oppression of women, cannot be discussed outside of its cultural religious context, in this case, Islam. What of the many women who argue that they wear the veil out of choice and say that in contrast to Western female dress (the purpose of which is to pander to the sexual desires of men), on the contrary preserves the dignity of the women, by covering them. It is a complex issue and no doubt many of us, western, eastern, northern and southern alike, rile at the sight of a fully clad women, whose eyes are the only visible part of her body. But it is not sufficient to call upon the logic of western radical and liberal feminism to reason the case.

Detachment and responsibility

The idea that data is a process of extraction implies that there is something static and objective in the research setting to be researched. Because we know that this is not the case it is therefore difficult to view the data collection process in terms of taking away something that belongs to someone or somewhere. However, we often feel like we are taking something away when we leave a research setting. Many of us are fortunate in that we are aided in our endeavour by generous people who we feel a tremendous responsibility towards. In overseas research, the proximity of the researcher to the researched in some sense is once removed. The researcher is not only often alien, in her/his relationship as researcher to the research subject, and from outside of the social setting, but is indeed often from a different culture. What makes the context of 'overseas' different than a situation of a person researching others from a different class (and thus in some ways a different culture)? Arguably, it is not simply the overseas researcher who is contextually 'alien' to the everyday workings of the researcher setting, but indeed any researcher/researched relationship in that the very 'act' of investigation produces an 'alienating' environment. Where the 'overseas' researcher has meaning in this discussion, is more to do with the culture of ideas than any national cultural difference. Much of the body of research conducted on the 'third-world' has come from scholars of the rich industrial north. It is in this tradition that the context of 'overseas' research/researcher takes on a particular meaning and in which reflexive and analytical care must be exercised.

The notion of detachment is inevitably tied up with that of responsibility and the expectations of the research subjects. The time old question is asked again here of whether we can be uninvolved as researchers. We are constantly being faced with and are forced to make decisions that may effect the lives of people we are working with. This may involve information we are holding or come across that may be important to our 'research participants'. Do we divulge this information? Indeed, do we actively become involved in seeking out ways which may alleviate the suffering (as we see it) of some of these people. Ultimately, do we have a moral responsibility to do this? What happens if they ask for help? Feminist approaches to research have sought to involve the researcher within the process thereby reducing the level of detachment. Involvement can be a part of the methodology because the information being sought requires it. Consciousness-raising is another step in this involvement and has been argued is a unique feminist method 'because it embodies principles such as enabling women to discuss and understand their experiences from their own viewpoints' (Reinharz, 1995:220). Indeed, when I serendipitously found a grant body that funds projects that the neighbourhood association in Brazil (with whom I was working) were pursuing, I presented the information to them and became involved in the application process.

The researcher has a responsibility to a number of different bodies and people. Often these obligations are conflictual and vary in their requirements. Not only are research subjects a consideration for the researcher, but so too are the funding bodies and other sponsors of the research and indeed the general social science community. Practically however, these considerations may become blurred. Faced with a dilemma, in a poor community, thousands of miles away from home, often the last consideration is the guidelines that your sponsor has laid down. Indeed, these guidelines may even seem irrelevant, out of touch and dictatorial.

Once back from the field and 'acclimatised' once more, it may all seem very different. This is not to undervalue the experience, but it may be that a combination of rules created from a distance have some function that mediates the often highly emotional experiences we have in the field. It is also the case that these experiences could be used more to enrich the texts that guide us on how to do research. This is where experience mediates the rules rather than the other way round. The only way we can truly come up with effective codes and guidelines is if experience is used directly to inform them.

The Brazilian context

The research project I have been concerned with for my doctoral thesis has involved work in Brazil, with women from a poor community who live on the periphery of an urban city in Brazil. In the main, the urban poor in Brazil live on the periphery of the large cities, with a high percentage of the population living in urban areas (three quarters of the Brazilian population, according to the 1991 census, IBGE 1995). The region in which I conducted my research project is the most impoverished in Brazil. The city of Salvador, where the project is centred is the capital of Bahia, the largest state in the region, and was the first capital of Brazil until it was moved to Rio and then later to Brasília.

The project's aim is to learn more about the experiences of women on the urban periphery and their experiences as poor urban women in a context of little government help and high unemployment. As a researcher from

Britain, my own personal connections with Brazil helped in building and consolidating ties with the Federal University of Bahia through which access to the community was gained.

My ethnic background gave me greater access to these women, via my colour and a proximity to some sort of Brazilian identity (i.e. knowledge of and involvement in popular culture). I certainly 'looked' familiar and unless I spoke, I was assumed to be Brazilian. This helped even when it was discovered that I was from somewhere else. The fact that I have brown skin (*morena*) meant that I was not obviously a 'gringa' (term used in Brazil for foreigner - usually from the U.S. or Europe). Of course, because I am not Brazilian, there was some trepidation as to what I was doing, and why I wanted information.

However, I tended to walk around the community (especially when I was interviewing) with someone from the neighbourhood association who would introduce me and sometimes sit with me during the interview. This helped get closer to the women and with how the interviewees responded. Because they tended to be generally relaxed, it was easier to have a discussion, which was the aim of the semi-structured approach. This can be contrasted to certain research projects that have taken place in the same area, where a 'group' of researchers and officials from Europe (Switzerland is one example) have walked around the neighbourhood and asked questions which has put the members of the community in a relatively uneasy situation. The atmosphere of detachment that this has produced has not helped gain the confidence of the people and community that is the subject of enquiry.

In the field

A number of interviews were carried out in the aim of discovering more about these women's lives and to learn about how they maintain themselves and families, as well as determining more about their context as mothers and carers in the community with comparatively little or no governmental help in terms of welfare. I was introduced to the community via a researcher in the Federal University. My first contact was with one of the organisers of a community association, which almost entirely consists of women (not uncommon in South America).[1]

After an initial meeting with the central members of the group, I was able to go into the wider community to interview women from the neighbourhood. Semi-structured interviews were adopted as a way of allowing space for the women who were being interviewed to interact with me (as the interviewer) and to ask questions of their own. It became clear on several occasions that some of the women, especially the one or two who were directly responsible for helping me with access to the women in the community, felt that I could help them monetarily. The woman who I spent most time with, inside the community (not part of the association), often asked me whether I could buy her a house on the other side of the neighbourhood, since her own was too small for herself and her two children.

'Overseas research' often involves a foreign researcher coming from a position of comparative economic superiority. As such, visits of this kind are frequently linked with the notion of aid. The expectation that the affluent visitor is there to provide help is one that can be seen in the expectations of various domains of the population that one is researching, from people within organisations to individuals in their homes. Research projects can thus raise the expectations of research subjects. We therefore have a responsibility to the research participant in that how we manage such expectations can effect the trust of the people we work with, not to mention any future projects that may require internal co-operation.

The neighbourhood association, of which I was closely connected by my second visit to Brazil, began to see me as a link between themselves and the 'outside world'. By this I mean that I, as foreign researcher from the developed world was seen as a natural contact with organisations that provide for ventures like theirs. They had already secured a grant from an international organisation for help to set up the community school from which they ran the association. Having spent a lot of time on a new project to set up the health centre and having already produced a report on their findings of a study about health issues in the community, their concern was how to fund it.

These women are far from helpless, oppressed and ignorant. On the contrary, they are vibrant, innovative and pro-active. In the face of lack of state help, their innovation pushes them to look beyond their borders. However, after I had suggested the grant that I had found, they began to enquire if I was aware of any other sources of finance that could be available for them, as their main grant was due to end in 2005 and they were also keen to set up a *Posto de Saude* (health centre) in the area. A number of considerations are important here including the issues of disclosure and responsibility. When I came across the grant that I realised would help the association in their endeavour to set up a health centre, I was faced with a dilemma. Should I disclose this grant to them, and indeed do I have a responsibility to disclose it to them given that I already had the knowledge that it existed, they were eligible and that if successfully won, would help their project of healthcare in their community. I chose not only to inform them of it, but to become involved in the application process.[2]

The conditions in which the community I worked within in Salvador lives, is one of extreme poverty. Many of the community's population, if they earn at all, earn less than the minimum salary (R$140), the equivalent of £50 per month. Many of the neighbourhood's inhabitants are unemployed or do *biscate* (odd-jobs) for a living, either through selling goods from home or small huts or by washing clothes or cleaning. Some are fortunate enough to find jobs that pay a minimum salary, often as maids to families nearer the centre of the city. This involves travelling on the bus in many cases for more than an hour to reach their destination. This work often begins very early in the morning, so an *empragada* (maid) would need to leave her own house at 5.00am or 6.00am to combat the morning traffic in order to arrive in time. Some *empragadas* live in, but some work only in the daytime and leave in the evening, sometimes very late around 7.00pm or 8.00pm. The northeast of the country still has a large live-in maid system unlike some other areas of the country especially in the more affluent south. There (in the south) maids, are increasingly choosing to work one or two days per week with one family and the rest with another, thereby increasing the possibility of a higher wage, receiving their salary daily rather than monthly, and having more control over themselves and their working times.

The women I interviewed were very responsive. I had only one refusal from the sixty-five women I interviewed in Brazil. The approach of a semi-structured interview style was chosen to give leeway to the women to respond and ask their own questions of me. I realised that my presence in the community was somewhat alien, but because I had been introduced to them by people from the *associação* (neighbourhood association), I was seen partially as an affiliate of the association.

Figure 6.1   **All in a Day's Work: woman cooking in her house**[3]

Figure 6.2   The Road Home[3]

The women I interviewed headed the households in which they lived. In this *bairro* (neighbourhood) of Salvador, many families are predominantly headed by a female. Moreover, these families are chiefly found amongst the poor in the third world (Castro, 1993). This is not to say that such families are solely dependant upon a single parent, as these mothers often have support from other people in the community via extended networks and family ties. They sometimes turn to their own mothers for help or close relatives or even other members of the community. Many of these women work *lavando para ganhar* (washing clothes for a living) or have jobs cleaning houses, or indeed sell goods from their houses or huts.

I worked in an area called the *alagados* which literally means 'flooded', because land has been filled where once before stood water and mangrove areas. The reason this land has been extended is because the people in this area found that there was not enough land to house them and thus they 'created' land or rather reclaimed the land from the sea to build upon. This is very often called an *invasão* (invasion), in Brazil, because in the most part it is taken by force or resistance. Consequently, many houses in this area are constructed on stilts where they have been built in the area of the mangrove when the filled land area was used up. Often, there was a danger in entering the area of the *palafitas* (the wooden shacks on stilts) as falling into the water would mean potentially contracting typhoid and other diseases. Indeed, even some of the people who lived in the immediate area were prone to falling in. However, they were very much more adept at walking what often seemed a tightrope, made of scanty wooden slats and poles for support, positioned sometimes two metres apart, so that the gap between them left you walking very carefully for fear of losing your balance. Many people in the neighbourhhood live in wooden shacks constructed with whatever material is available to them. Often these houses are not complete in that they still need part of the roof completed or they require walls fortified. Some houses are *construida* (constructed from brick) and are more solid. These houses tend to be located on the filled land of further into the centre of the neighbourhood, where there is solid ground to support them.

Figure 6.3   **A Child's World: boy with his family outside their house**[3]

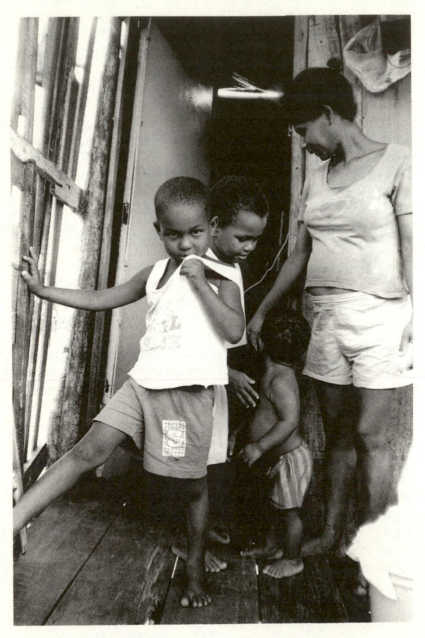

Figure 6.4   Making Do: entrance to a house on the Palafitas[3]

My status as a researcher who was connected to the university in Salvador was a remote and distant concept for many of the women I interviewed. In addition, my proximity to the neighbourhood association, again little of whose activities had been heard of, was ambiguous. I was a person from a distant place (Britain), and I came to realise that this in some ways alleviated any anxiety the women may have had, since any information that they would impart would not be seen by anyone who knew them or any members of their community. On the other hand, there was a sense of trust because I was being introduced by women of the association, some of whom were known to them. My foreign accent was a constant reminder that although I may look Brazilian (even northeastern), that I was from elsewhere, an elsewhere that was even further removed than the middle class and detached areas of the city in which they lived. Nevertheless, often the women would chat to me on a level that sometimes revealed experiences that were very painful for them to talk about, such as a child who had left for São Paulo, in the richer south of the country, and who had not written or communicated since, or in one case the violent abuse that one women had suffered by her husband, that even the women from the association were not aware of. Trust therefore became the linchpin, certainly with my relationship with the women from the neighbourhood associations and with those who began recognising me.

Conclusion

Although this chapter was originally entitled 'Beyond the Borders of Research; Ethical Considerations in Overseas Fieldwork', it quickly became apparent that what I wanted to talk about had more to do with ideological categories, born from geographical and cultural comparatives than the issue of a spatial divide. This further caused me to contemplate the use of the term *overseas*, in the title. The idea of overseas can be seen in the most part as a term that has come to represent research of the developing world initiated by the developed world. Therefore the meanings that are attached to it have connotations associated with relations of power and the rise of hegemonic spheres of ideas.

The objective of the study cited was to discover more about the lives of women in a poor community who rely on little or no governmental support and who in the main are responsible for finding resources to feed their children, themselves and the maintenance of the household. Trust was a crucial factor in my work in the neighbourhood in Salvador, and this concept goes beyond the rather scant definition of confidence of information, consent and privacy. Rather it incorporates a complex labyrinth of meanings within the research setting. The context of the researcher in relation to the setting and what informs the ideas that are taken to the setting, bear heavily on the way in which the social relations of that setting will be understood. Responsibility to our research participants extends beyond the ethical considerations of the right to be asked to participate, to a responsibility towards representing the social relations we are studying outside of predefined categories. Paradoxes arise from an assumption that it is not possible to have a set of criteria ordered and functioning in a manner that falls outside of preconceived expectations.

Despite vast amounts of literature discussing the incidence of pro-action of women within poor communities in South America it has been difficult to account for *why*. The powerful image of the icon of the Virgin Mary originating from Catholicism and often attributed to the rationale of *Marianismo* in South America, in which the pure, family abiding female fulfils her dutiful role as mother and good wife, is one which women have been complicit in and have fulfilled and appropriated for themselves. Thus the idea that women should be organising on a political level, by themselves and within the private sphere choosing to leave the marital home represents a break from this. Recent research has shown that we are able to see that such action can be attributed to the idea that motherhood is challenging those stereotypes (Neuhouser, 1998). Women thus feel that their role as mother has particular meaning and that if circumstances require it, it is necessary to break other norms such as staying in and tending for the house in order to fulfil that role. In addition the way that role is being defined by women themselves is changing as necessity and circumstances within poverty affects it (Makkar, 1999). Thus, the so called 'paradox' dissipates when values, and even cultural nuances are examined in their context.

Ultimately we have a responsibility to produce research which does not adopt an ethnocentric universality that assumes itself to be the defining measure by which to view social relations and practices.

Notes

1. Researchers of women in Latin America have recognised this as a striking aspect of popular movements in poor communities in South America (Alvarez, 1990; Caldeira, 1990; Machado, 1993).

2. Some eighteen months after the application for the grant was made, the association was awarded the total requested funds to establish the health centre and it is now providing a basic service to the immediate community.

3. Photographs © Bani Dev Makkar.

References

Alvarez, S. (1990) 'Women's Participation in the Brazilian "People's Church": A Critical Appraisal'. *Feminist Studies* 16 (Summer): 381-408.

Associação de Moradores Do Conjunto Santa Luzia. (1996) *Projeto Especial Santa Luzia: Uma Proposta de Intervenção em Saúde no Bairro do Urugai.* Unpublished Report. Salvador: Bahia.

Bulmer, M. (ed.) (1982) *Social Research Ethics.* Macmillan: London.

Caldeira, T.P.R. (1990) 'Women, Daily Life and Politics'. In *Women and Social Change in Latin America*, ed. Elizabeth Jelin, 47-78. UNRISD/ Zed Books: London.

Castro, M. (1993) "Similarities and Differences: Female Headed Households in Brazil an Colombia" in Joan P. Mencher and Anne Okongwn (eds.) *Where Did All the Men Go?: Female-Headed/Female Supported Households in Cross-Cultural Perspective*, 132-169. Westview Press: London.

DaMatta, R. (1995) 'For an Anthropology of the Brazilian Tradition' or 'A Virtude está no Meio' in David J. Hess and Roberto A. DaMatta (eds.) *The Brazilian Puzzle; Culture on the Borderlands of the Western World*, 270-291. Columbia University Press: New York.

Instituto Brasileiro de Geografia e Estatístico (IBGE) (1995) Anuário Estatístico do Brasil. Rio de Janeiro: IBGE.

Kimmel, A.J. (1988), *Ethics and Values in Applied Social Research.* California: Sage Publications.

Machado, L.M.V. (1993) 'We Learned to Think Politically: The influence of the Catholic Church and the feminist movement on the emergence of the health movement of the Jardim Nordeste area in São Paulo, Brazil" in Sarah A. Radcliffe and Sallie Westwood (eds.) *Viva, Women and Popular Protest in Latin America*, 88-111: Routledge.

Makkar, B.D. (1999) *Life on the Edge: Survival Strategies of Women in the Urban Periphery in Salvador, Brazil.* Paper presented at the 19th

International Conference of the Annual ILASSA Conference on Latin America, University of Texas at Austin, 26-27 February 1999.

May, T. (1993) *Social Research; Issues, Methods and Process.* Buckingham: Open University Press.

Mohanty, C. T. (1991) 'Under Western Eyes: Feminist Scholarship and Colonial Discourses' in Chandra Talpade Mohanty, Ann Russo and Lourdes Torres (eds.) *Third World Women and the Politics of Feminism*, 51-81. Bloomington: Indiana University Press.

Neuhouser, K. (1998) '"If I had Abandoned My Children": Community Mobilization and Commitment to the Identity of Mother in Northeast Brazil'. *Social Forces.* 77(1): 331-358.

Oakley, A. (1981) 'Interviewing women: a contradiction in terms' in Helen Roberts (ed.) *Doing Feminist Research*, 30-61. London: Routledge and Kegan Paul.

Reinharz, S. (1992) *Feminist Methods in Social Research.* Oxford: Oxford University Press.

7 Your place or mine? Ethics, the researcher and the Internet

KATE ROBSON AND MARK ROBSON

Uses of CMCs in social research

This chapter outlines the areas of consideration that are relevant to the use of computer mediated communications for collecting qualitative social research data. It is now fairly common for computer mediated communications (CMC's) to be used in order to administer quantitative social research. It offers a quick, cheap and convenient alternative to mailing questionnaires, and is often associated with a more favourable response rate than paper-based equivalents (Selwyn and Robson, 1998a). However, increasingly, the social sciences have been harnessing CMCs as a topic of and a tool for qualitative research too. In looking at qualitative computer mediated social research it is worth distinguishing between research that has looked at computerised communications as a topic of study, and research that has used computerised communications as a tool for conducting qualitative research (Selwyn and Robson 1998b). Of course there's going to be a great deal of overlap between these. In order to undertake any kind of study of computer mediated communities, it's more than likely that you're going to use these communications to conduct this research. However, computerised communications are becoming so widespread and so mainstream, that research that uses the technology no longer has to primarily 'be about' the technology.

So, we see examples of ethnographies of specific online communities, observations of communities (e.g. Baym, 1995; Paccagnella, 1997), content analysis of bodies of e-mails (e.g. Hoch et al. 1997). And in addition to studies like those, there are the studies using the technology as a tool – questionnaires aren't the only research tool that can be used in a computer mediated version. Interviews can be conducted, either in real time using chat software, or by e-mail correspondence (Selwyn and Robson, 1998a).

94

Focus groups can be set up (Murray, 1997; Robson, 1998), which differ from the study of existing online discussions in that they have been set up and recruited specifically for a study.

Embracing computerised communications in social research is appealing - it's topical, it's interesting, and it's relatively easy to do - it's quick, it's cheap. You can reach widespread populations from the comfort of your office, and you don't have to transcribe your data. These features are tempting, but before rushing headlong into any such research, a fresh eye must be cast over otherwise familiar regulations relating to behaviour and research practice.

These considerations must take account of two fields of the regulation of behaviour: codes of conduct that relate to behaviour in computer mediated groups and communities, and codes of conduct relating to the practice of social research. It is necessary to be acquainted with, and to consider both of these areas when engaging in social research that utilises these media. Ethical issues are always problematic in any traditional research setting or approach, and in a relatively new social, communications or research environment, where conventions are still emerging, they are all the more so. This chapter will first outline relevant issues arising from acceptable and expected behaviour in computerised communications, and then address the ethics of conducting social research. The aim of this chapter is to present together issues relating to conduct from these two areas that social researchers engaging in computer mediated settings should consider before embarking on their research.

Internet codes of conduct

How we use the Internet and what is deemed as acceptable behaviour is not governed by a single organisation or body but rather through an amalgam of service providers' acceptable use policies, codes of conduct and the implications of certain laws. Acceptable use policies refer to the agreement that is made between the user and the service provider, and these contractual agreements generally include acceptable and unacceptable use policies that to some degree define how the user can use the network. Codes of conduct refer to the informal codes of conduct that have been developed over time and adopted by the online community - what has become known as 'netiquette'. These codes of conduct along with civil rights and cyber rights issues are continually being discussed, developed and defended by the online community through bodies or organisations like Computer

Professionals for Social Responsibility (CPSR) and the Electronic Frontier Foundation (EFF). Certain laws have some implications for how we use the Internet as well, for example data protection and privacy laws. Although the contracts with the service providers and the laws are the most structured, the more informal codes of conduct (netiquette) seem to hold more weight especially for what is deemed as acceptable behaviour. This is in part because they have been created by the community itself, and more probably because they are more widely known about and understood than the acceptable use policies.

Acceptable use policies (AUP's)

Internet service providers' acceptable use policies and terms of use are probably the most structured control of how we use the Internet specifically, although for most people they are probably only a page they clicked past when setting up their connection and have never thought of since. They do however give the service provider some control over the way you use the Internet when accessing it via their network. They are largely fairly similar in what they cover, outlining what is and isn't allowed on the particular network generally with a strong emphasis on responsible use of the network and not doing anything that would have an effect on the availability of the network to others. Most include a statement that says when you use the network to access any other network or services the AUP's, terms and conditions of those networks will also apply to you. With regards to research they give no specific guidance although key points are of relevance to this discussion. Notably, regulations such as these illustrated by the following examples relate to issues of privacy and protection from harm.

For example, MITNET's (Massachusetts Institute of Technology) Rules of Use state that
- 'All members of the MIT community are obligated to use these facilities in accordance with applicable laws, with Institute standards of honesty and personal conduct, and in ways that are responsible, ethical, and professional'.
- 'All users of MITnet should make sure that their actions don't violate the privacy of other users, if even unintentionally' including – *'Don't try to intercept or otherwise monitor any network communications not explicitly intended for you'*.

JANET (which is the British universities' 'backbone') has a list of unacceptable uses in its AUP which includes:

- '9.2 the creation or transmission of material which is designed or likely to cause annoyance, inconvenience or needless anxiety'.
- '9.7 deliberate activities with any of the following characteristics: violating the privacy of others'.

Netiquette

Informal codes of conduct were developed naturally by the online community as the Internet grew and developed. They outline standard practises for the various services available over the Internet (e-mail, newsgroups, IRC etc.) and define how to behave and what is unacceptable behaviour within these areas. These codes have become known as netiquette and are (or should be) required reading for anyone new to the Internet. Netiquette includes specific guidelines or etiquette for the different services that are available over the Internet such as e-mail netiquette or newsgroup netiquette. The document RFC1855, which was produced by the Responsible Use of the Network Working Group of the Internet Engineering Task Force (IETF) provides a minimum set of netiquette guidelines, in a format that allows organisations to take and adapt it for their own use. It covers one-to-one communication, one-to-many communication and information services. Within these guidelines there is a strong emphasis on observing the guidelines and culture, of the group or medium you are participating in. It also highlights the fact that the Internet is a global community made up of people representing a diversity of cultures, religions and lifestyles that users should be tolerant of. Examples of these guidelines that have specific relevance to this discussion are

- in one to one communication (e-mail) section 'In general, rules of common courtesy for interaction with people should be in force for any situation and on the Internet it's doubly important where, for example, body language and tone of voice must be inferred'.
- 'Any time you engage in One-to-Many communications, all the rules for mail should also apply. After all, communicating with many people via one mail message or post is quite analogous to communicating with one person with the exception of possibly offending a great many more people than in one-to-one communication. Therefore, its quite important to know as much as you can about the audience of your message'.
- 'Some mailing lists are private. Do not send mail to these lists uninvited. Do not report mail from these lists to a wider audience'.

- in Information Services section (which includes WWW, MUDs, and IRC). 'Tell users what you plan to do with any information you collect, such as WWW feedback. You need to warn people if you plan to publish any of their statements, even passively by just making it available to other users'.

There are many guides to netiquette available on the worldwide web. They all cover roughly the same things, providing guidelines for behaviour on the Internet and offering advice on how to use certain features or services. A highly referenced and linked to one of these is Rinaldi's publication The Net: User Guidelines and Netiquette. This emphasises that the policies and terms of the networks being used should be followed, and that any use that is unlawful, or would cause congestion of the networks, or otherwise interfere with the work of others is unacceptable. Included in this guide are the ten commandments from the Computer Ethics Institute which are

1   Thou shalt not use a computer to harm other people.
2. Thou shalt not interfere with other people's computer work.
3. Thou shalt not snoop around in other people's files.
4. Thou shalt not use a computer to steal.
5. Thou shalt not use a computer to bear false witness.
6. Thou shalt not use or copy software for which you have not paid.
7. Thou shalt not use other people's computer resources without authorization.
8. Thou shalt not appropriate other people's intellectual output.
9. Thou shalt think about the social consequences of the program you write.
10. Thou shalt use a computer in ways that show consideration and respect.

Beyond broader general netiquette guides many of the communities that have formed on the Internet around things like chat rooms or newsgroups have created there own specific set of rules or guidelines (in addition to the broader netiquette) that apply just to that particular chat room or newsgroup. As with the IETF guidelines discussed above most of the general guides to netiquette refer to these indicating that they should be read and followed.

The law

Legal issues relating to the use of computerised communications are complex, and a comprehensive review of these is beyond the scope of this chapter. There are a variety of laws internationally that relate to the use of computers and communication technology. For example in Britain there is the Data Protection Act 1988 and the Computer Misuse Act 1990. The laws that are of particular relevance to this discussion are primarily the data protection and privacy laws. The Data Protection Act states that if you are storing personal information about people on a computer then you must have adequate security in place to protect that data and you must be registered. Clearly this will apply to a large amount of research projects as they often involve storing personal data on a computer. Although attention to legal issues pertaining to computerised communications is important, in general term, adherence to AUP's and netiquette will usually meet with legal requirements.

Organisations

Covering all of the areas outlined above, organisations like the Internet Society, Computer Professional for Social Responsibility and the Electronic Frontier Foundation, along with many others, work on behalf of the online community to maintain the Internet as a free open global community available and beneficial to all. Along these lines they are involved in the continuous evolution and development of online codes of conduct such as netiquette and with the development of any regulations or laws that have a direct impact on the use of the Internet both through working with the relevant government bodies and through campaigning. They are also highly involved in the use of the Internet and it implications on an individual's civil rights or what has become known as cyber rights. Along with freedom of speech an individual's right to privacy and anonymity are the big cyber rights issue with these organisations actively campaigning to establish and defend an individual's right to these on the Internet. For example the CPSR have produced a set of electronic privacy guidelines, which advocates that individuals should be made aware of any policies to do with the collection of personal information and what that information will be used for. In conclusion it states that 'the ethical responsibility for privacy protection lies with those who would violate that privacy, and with those who design and provide the systems where the violations can occur'.

Ethics in social research

Ethical concerns don't just arise at the margins of research, as a tendency to concentrate on extreme examples in literature on research ethics may often imply. Ethical issues and dilemmas are almost universally encountered, and may involve any actor at any stage of the research process (Rees, 1991). The central issues of professional and ethical codes of conduct that have been developed for social research (e.g. British Sociological and American Sociological Association guidelines) generally relate to issues of informed consent, of privacy, confidentiality and dignity, of the avoidance of harm (Punch, 1986). Previous considerations of ethical issues of computer mediated research have tended to focus on the issue of privacy, and have too often been justificatory exercises, intellectualising what, in an equivalent terrestrial setting, would be considered intrusive and unacceptable research practice.

Informed consent

Informed consent is constituted of three elements: firstly the responsibility of the researcher to ensure the participants' understanding of what participation in the research will involve; secondly that participants are not coerced into participating; and finally that participants are truly free to review their decision to participate and withdraw their participation at any point (Smith, 1975). It is the researcher's responsibility to ensure that explanations are appropriate for potential participants, and groups who are more vulnerable to exploitation especially warrant suitable and thorough explanations.

Seeking consent from those who are recruited for computer mediated interviewing, or a 'virtual focus group' set up for research purposes is relatively straightforward and comparable to eliciting consent in more traditional situations. However, as with any covert research, studies that observe naturally occurring computer communities, or that 'plant' questions in existing discussion groups face a more problematic situation. Because of the sometimes intermittent nature of participants' engagement in computer mediated settings, in order that information explaining the presence of the researcher is seen by all who pass through, such information would have to be regularly repeated. However, such repetitions may interfere too greatly with the natural interactions of the group, and flout conventions of repetition in discussions.

'Harvesting' - the collection of material from computer mediated interactions without prior consent - is viable and legal, and may be attractive as a speedy and easy way of collecting rich data. However, to many Internet users, such research would be unethical according to the conventions of the medium (Sharf, 1999). The B.S.A's ethical guidelines for social research do countenance obtaining post-hoc consent where gaining prior consent may have been impracticable, but should be relied on with caution, as it may not appease the objections of those users who disapprove of harvesting. Nonetheless, gaining consent to use computer mediated material is imperative, and a contributory factor in this is the fact that regardless of how users perceive their communications in terms of privacy and intimacy, the nature of their articulation may determine them as published material. It is therefore simply not enough to gain the consent of 'gatekeepers' (sysops, channel ops, list managers etc.).

Privacy, confidentiality and anonymity

Ostensibly the idea that identifying information should be kept confidential for the purposes of any written report of the research seems fairly straightforward. However, the risk of deductive disclosure is very real in research in computerised communities. Most texts that review the ethics of research rehearse a few familiar, 'notorious' cases that were ethically problematic. The 'Springdale Case' of the 1950's is usually among these. In this small-town community, the identities of locals (especially the few local officials) were virtually impossible to conceal, because the possibilities of who these pseudonymised characters might really be were so limited. As a result, the participants in the project were left feeling angry and betrayed by the research process (Becker, 1978; Smith, 1975). Arguably, the Internet is a computerised nation of cyber-Springdales, where in order to retain their character and viability, small towns never grow into metropolises, instead spawning more small towns, each in some way characteristically distinct from the other. Yes, there are, for example, newsgroups to cover just about every aspect of human interest, but *how many* are there for each. To describe and convey the character of a computer mediated community or group, in so very many cases, is to identify it in all but name.

But even if you can effectively disguise the setting, problems are still encountered with regard to affording anonymity and confidentiality. Complete anonymity is, of course, almost impossible to guarantee, as information about the origin of a computer transmitted message is for most users, almost impossible to remove. The absence of anonymity in research doesn't of course mean researchers can't guarantee confidentiality to research subjects. However in computer mediated research, this is more difficult to do. Traditional procedures for storage of data and anonymising participants are complicated in a medium where a *record of the original data* is routinely available to others who have participated in the research -

members of a distribution list discussion for example. Any research quoting or explicitly referring to an article posted in any kind of group discussion can not prevent the identification of the author of that message by others. In a traditional, terrestrial group research setting, in order for any one participant to retain a copy of the original data requires conscious decision and great effort to secure that. In the computer mediated research setting, conscious decision is required to *not* have such a record. As such, the ASA's statement of ethical practice that holds that researchers should *'prevent data being published or released in a form which would permit the actual or potential identification of research participants'* is virtually impossible to adhere to.

Much of this issue depends on definitions of computer mediated communications being private or public forms of communication. Arguably, different kinds of online media differ in terms of their perceived degree of privacy that are afforded to them in their use. Privacy can occur within public situations (Elgesem, cited in Sharf, 1999), and crucially, because these communications are often perceived as private *by users*, greater intimacy and self-revelation is encouraged (Sharf, 1999). Where the conventions of the setting define privacy, so should the researcher respect that definition, and act accordingly, regardless of how the argument of privacy can be intellectualised independently of the research setting. The definition of the privacy of the encounters should always be case specific, and dependent on the perception of the level of privacy on the part of the participant. Nonetheless, in general terms of what online is private and what is public, we would suggest that a continuum of increasing privacy operates, which is informally understood by most users. Websites and open access message boards are most publicly situated, with other forms of discussion suggesting increasing degrees of privacy determined by how readily they can be read or contributed to, with one-to-one real-time or asynchronous communications suggesting the greatest level of privacy.

Paccagnella's (1997) much cited analogy of all computer mediated communications being like 'letters to the editor' or tombstone inscriptions, as personal but not private, has served to legitimise many research behaviours in this field that we contend to be irresponsible and unethical. Because issues of the privacy of computer mediated communications are so often treated in isolation from other ethical issues in computer mediated research, issues such as the emotional distress to research subjects caused by such an opinion of all computerised communications, remain obscured. Using Paccagnella's (1997) 'personal not private' stance, outlined above, Smyres (1999) joined and observed an online community of adolescent girls, collecting, analysing and reporting unpseudonymised postings made by the girls seeking advice about their bodies from the other members of the community. Although the site operates a degree of privacy for its members, requiring registration in order to either read or contribute to such discussions, Smyres neither asked the girls' permission to report their highly personal messages, nor even informed them that she would. She even acknowledges that such a study of teenagers in a terrestrial setting raised ethical problems, and would be impossible: 'I wanted them to be in a safe space, one that they had specifically chosen, and one where they felt comfortable to speak their minds' (Smyres 1999:3). It seems that all too often, researchers adopt a far more cavalier attitude to research subjects that they can not see, hear or touch, than they would to participants engaged in more traditional forms of research.

Protection from harm

Persisting with a definition of 'public', however intellectually defensible, that is at odds with the one in the setting risks causing emotional harm or distress to participants. Participation in social research should not introduce any unnecessary hazards: any known or foreseeable risks must be outweighed by the potential or probable benefits of the research findings (Smith, 1975). To this end, only relevant data should be gathered, and it should be stored securely. Again, however diligently the researcher does this, they can have no ultimate control over material that will have been retained by any participants in the research, restricting the ability of the researcher to protect the researched from harm. Informing potential participants about the research to elicit consent to participate isn't merely about explaining the research procedure, it must include information about the foreseeable uses to which the research findings will be put. But the ability to do this will inevitably be undermined in a setting where the research process and data can be so easily shared by others.

Reciprocity

Finally, to this list of ethical considerations of research, we would add ethical responsibilities to share or disseminate findings of research to the people who have been researched. In many ways, this may be seen as the corollary of responsibility to protect participants from harm: not only should research *not harm* participants, but it should *benefit* them also. The idea that research is a two way process which should benefit both the researcher and the researched is no longer a principle confined to academic feminism, where it had its roots (Reinharz, 1983). Clearly the ease and speed with which information can be transmitted and shared lends itself to the fulfilment of this. Data can be reviewed and reflected on by participants in a way much easier to conduct than in traditional, terrestrial research, where such tasks are time consuming and costly, and practical constraints of doing research may prevent the fulfilment of such good intentions. Arguably again, the ethos of computer mediated communities contributes to the importance that should be placed on realising principles relating to this issue: principles of non-hierarchical information sharing that pervade such communities make the sharing and dissemination of research findings to participant groups more important and appropriate.

Conclusion: Guidance on ethical conduct in computer mediated social research

The purpose of this chapter is not to offer a set of rules that all computer mediated social research should adhere to, but rather to raise the issues from the two relevant fields of codes of conduct that researchers in this field should consider. All research settings, both in the 'real' and 'virtual' worlds, are unique, and the process of researching in any setting is always characterised by best efforts and compromise. Ethical codes of conduct are only ever benchmarks to gauge ethical issues surrounding a particular research setting, and are always, realistically, as unattainable as any ideal type (Punch, 1986; Smith, 1975). Acknowledged weaknesses in one area (e.g. informed consent) can often arguably be compensated for in other areas, such as increased importance on confidentiality and protection from harm (Barnard, 1992). The lack of consideration of a breadth of ethical issues raised by both the fields covered here is a notable failing of previous considerations of the ethics of computer mediated research. It seems that so much has been invested in the creation and defence of the absolute public status of computerised communications, that other issues have been neglected.

Given the ease with which computer mediated social research can be undertaken, it is important to highlight all of the areas that may be ethically problematic and require forethought, before rushing into any such research. So rather than guidelines, we offer a number of areas that should be questioned before embarking on a project.

1. *The collection of naturally occurring interactions without consent should be avoided wherever possible.*
    Can interactions be 'siphoned off' into one-to-one or groups interviews for the research?
    Will relying on post-hoc consent be acceptable to the researched group, or may it damage opportunities for future researchers?
    Are there gatekeepers that should be approached before participants?

2. *Privacy, anonymity and confidentiality are always going to be much harder for the researcher to retain control of than in traditional research settings.*
    Can these be achieved?
    Is this 'Springdale', can deductive disclosure be guarded against?
    What extra efforts can be made to protect participants from harm?
    Can alternative computer mediated data collection tools be used to minimise threats to privacy, anonymity and confidentiality?
    Do your perceptions of what is private match those you meet in the setting, or do *you* need to reconsider?

3. *Protection from harm.*
    Who else may have received copies of the original data through the research process?
    In cases of virtual focus groups, can you seek assurances from members to respect the confidentiality of the data?
    Are participants aware of how widely and easily information they contributed to your research may be disseminated by others? Are you aware of this?

4. *Take advantage of the greater opportunities to share your research findings.*
    In computer mediated research environments, it's relatively quick and easy, and there is no excuse not to. Be open to participants' comments and corrections about how you represented them, as ultimately this will offer you and the wider research community greater understanding of the field.

The conduct of sociological research using these new forms of communication requires a revisiting of traditional principles of ethical conduct of research. To suggest that 'old' ethical principles need not or can not be applied in online communities is both intellectually and methodologically lazy. The issues that we have outlined here can be applied in this new medium in a way that need not stifle the development of valuable sociological research.

Notes

American Sociological Association Code of Ethics
   http://www.asanet.org/ecoderev.htm
British Sociological Association Statement of Ethical Practice
   http://dialspace.dial.pipex.com/town/parade/ot36/ethgu2.htm
CPSR Privacy Guidelines
   http://www.cpsr.org/program/privacy/privacy8.htm
Guidelines for the Data Protection Act
   http://www.open.gov.uk/dpr/dprhome.htm
JANET's Acceptable Use Policy *http://www.ja.net/documents/use.html*
MITNET Rules of Use *http://web.mit.edu/olh/Welcome/rules.html#mitnet*
RFC1855 *http://www.cis.ohio-state.edu/htbin/rfc/rfc1855.html*

References

Barnard, M. (1992) Working in the Dark: researching female prostitution. In Roberts (Ed.), *Women's Health Matters*. London: Routledge.

Baym, N. (1995) From Practice to Culture on Newsnet. In S. Star (Ed.), *The Cultures of Computing*. Oxford: Blackwell.

Becker, H. (1978) Problems in the Publication of Field Studies. In Bynner and Stribley (Eds.), *Social Research: Principles and Procedures*. Harlow: Longman.

Hoch, D., Norris, D., Lester, J., and Marcus, A. (1997). Information Exchange in an Epilepsy Forum on the World Wide Web [http://neuro-oas.mgh.harvard.edu/cscw98/seizure_paper.html].

Murray, P. (1997) Using Virtual Focus Groups in Qualitative Research. *Qualitative Health Research*, November 1997.

Paccagnella, L. (1997) Getting the Seats of Your Pants Dirty: Strategies for Ethnographic Research on Virtual Communities. *Journal of Computer Mediated Communication*, 3.

Punch, M. (1986) *The Politics and Ethics of Fieldwork*. Beverly Hills: Sage.

Rees, T. (1991) Ethical Issues. In Allen and Skinner (Eds.), *Handbook for Research Students in the Social Sciences*. London: Falmer.

Reinharz, S. (1983) Experiential analysis: a contribution to feminist research. In G. Bowles and R. Klein (Eds.), *Theories of Women's Studies*. London: Routledge and Kegan Paul.

Rinaldi, A.H. (1996) The Net: User Guidelines and Netiquette *http://www.fau.edu/rinaldi/net/index.html*

Robson, K. (1998) Meat in the Machine: the centrality of the body in Internet interactions. In A. Shaw and J. Richardson (Eds.), *The Body in Qualitative Research*. Aldershot: Ashgate.

Selwyn, N. and Robson, K. (1998a) Using Email as a Research Tool, *Social Research Update, 21 http://www.soc.surrey.ac.uk/sru/sru21.html*

Selwyn, N. and Robson, K. (1998b) *Using Electronic Mail as a Research Tool in Education and the Social Sciences*, Working Paper 29, Cardiff: School of Education.

Sharf, B. (1999) Beyond Netiquette: The Ethics of Doing Naturalistic Discourse Research on the Internet. In S. Jones (Ed.), *Doing Internet Research*. Thousand Oaks: Sage.

Smith, H. (1975) *Strategies of Social Research: The Methodological Imagination*. London: Prentice Hall.

Smyres, K (1999) Virtual Corporeality: Adolescent Girls and Their Bodies in Cyberspace, *Cybersociology, 6.*
http://www.socio.demon.co.uk/magazine/6/smyres.html

8 Reflections on fieldwork in criminal justice institutions

CATRIN SMITH AND EMMA WINCUP

The importance of ethical issues (along with such topics as emotions and 'gender') in ethnographic fieldwork has increasingly been recognised in recent years. While the focus of criticism has traditionally been on the issue of covert research and the violation of principles of consent, there is now a growing body of literature highlighting the (often) unanticipated ethical dilemmas in overt field research (Norris, 1993). Both May (1993) and Norris (1993) point to the importance of critical reflection and dialogue in social research. May (1993:56) suggests that this may be where an ethical code has value: to enable 'the researcher to continually reflect on the expectations which they make of people and their relationships with those party to the research'.

In what follows we focus on some of the ethical dilemmas we encountered as postgraduate researchers and the ways in which our experiences in the field forced us to reflect on our research practice, as researchers in training and as self-consciously feminist women. We highlight the research strategies we developed in order to deal with the situational complexities of sensitive research, and the consequences of our actions (where known).

The researches

The authors were both Ph.D. students when the researches under discussion were carried out. Both projects were conducted in the mid-1990s and both were concerned with the particular experiences of women who appear before the courts, but at different stages of the criminal justice process. The first (Wincup, 1997) focused on women awaiting trial, a group that has rarely been researched. The study aimed to capture the neglected experiences of staff and residents within bail hostels by highlighting the needs of women awaiting trial and analysing the ways in which hostels aim to offer them support as well as the barriers to the provision of that support. In contrast, women's prisons have been relatively well researched and there have been important studies which have raised awareness of the particular experiences of women in prison (see, Howe, 1994, for a review). However, an overlooked aspect in this work has been the relationship between women's imprisonment and women's health. The second study (Smith, 1996), while concerned with women's experiences of imprisonment generally, thus sought to explore the health problems and needs of women in prison and the patterns of institutional response.

While distinct in terms of the research focus, the two projects were practically, theoretically and methodologically similar. Both pieces of work were qualitative, exploratory studies combining a semi-participant approach with in-depth, semi-structured interviews with those living and working in women's bail hostels and prisons. Both studies were informed by overlapping theoretical positions, particularly debates within feminists' criminology. We use the term 'feminist criminology' to emphasise that there are many feminisms, while recognising that both feminism and criminology are diverse, fragmented disciplines.

In the 1970s and for some time, feminist concern was directed at the misrepresentation and/or the absence and invisibility of women in conventional criminological research (see, for example, Smart, 1976). Later studies, however, rejected this essentialist stance and sought to explore the relationship between gender and other social divisions such as ethnicity, social class and age (Rice, 1990; Smart, 1990). Hence, while our researches focused on an exploration of women's experiences in criminal justice institutions, we remained sensitive to the diversity of those experiences. Of central importance to the feminist research agenda has been the need to focus on the complexities and problems of women's situations and the institutions that influence those situations (Olesen, 1998).

As is the case with academic apprenticeships such as these, both studies were solo enterprises conducted against the clock (with lesser and greater degrees of supervision) involving in-depth prolonged periods of immersion in the field. Both involved 'captive', vulnerable populations and, in both studies, careful consideration was given to ethical issues prior to entering the field and the researches designed accordingly. However, criminal justice institutions are unlike many other research settings and our approach to our research practice was keenly shaped by our experiences in the field and the range of (anticipated and unanticipated) situational and institutional factors we encountered.

Negotiating access

Physically getting in to criminal justice institutions, particularly prisons, for research purposes is no easy task and much depends upon the nature of the research and how it and the researcher are perceived by the official gatekeepers (see Liebling, 1992; Smartt, 1995; Smith, 1996). As Cohen and Taylor (1972) have highlighted, prisoners, like other captive populations, are to all intents and purposes the 'property' of the state and we were both dependent, to greater and lesser degrees, on getting the official go-ahead to conduct our researches. In the prison context this generally needs to be obtained in the first instance from the Home Office and subsequently through the prison Governor and in bail hostels it needs to be secured through the Chief Probation Officer and then the hostel manager. Both pieces of work were conducted at a particularly sensitive time in penal politics and we were both keenly aware that we had to tread carefully in our dealings with the formal gatekeepers and present ourselves as non-threatening individuals so as to maximise our chances of gaining access. However, the strategies needed to do this - for example, through the expression of understanding of the gatekeeper's perspective - at times conflicted with our values as feminist researchers and, in particular, as academics self-consciously attempting to investigate sympathetically the experiences of women labelled 'criminal'. While we do not feel that we deceived our gatekeepers, it is certainly true that the researcher selves we presented were shaped by what we thought would be acceptable to the person/people we were with at the time so as to gain access. At each level different dimensions of the research were highlighted or downplayed accordingly.

For a range of possible reasons we neither of us had any real problems in gaining access to our research establishments: three bail hostels (Wincup, 1997) and three women's prisons (Smith, 1996). However, the process of negotiating access with our gatekeepers proved to be much more time-consuming than we had originally anticipated. Furthermore, while no explicit constraints were imposed on either piece of research, for one of us (CS) an on-going informal *quid pro quo* relationship with a key gatekeeper who was particularly interested in the data raised certain ethical concerns. These were overcome by the researcher adhering as far as possible to issues of anonymity and confidentiality, whilst periodically providing the gatekeeper with research reports.

The issue of social access and the strategies for 'getting on' after 'getting in' are highly personal experiences offering few means of preparation for novice researchers. In both projects we were continuously being 'sussed out' in relation to formal and informal criteria. We were well aware that the existence of internal frictions could have jeopardised our researches. We were also aware that the (top-down) decisions about access were made without the consultation of the many other groups being studied. This raised a number of concerns for us about acceptance in the field and the development of rapport and relationships. We had, after all been permitted access at a difficult time, politically, and, quite rightly, both prison and hostel staff and the women prisoners and residents wondered why (were we spies?). Moreover, it was not our intention for our observations to become covert. In order to overcome some of these problems we both spent lengthy periods at the outset of the research getting our faces known and generally explaining who we were and why we were interested in their lives (see Smith and Wincup, forthcoming, for a more detailed discussion).

Institutional research and the thorny issue of informed consent

In both projects, participants were given full explanations about our research intentions, who was financing the projects (both were supported by university studentships), why they were being undertaken and how the results were to be disseminated. At times, we struggled to find a common language to explain clearly the aims of the research and why their involvement was desirable. We assured participants of their right to refuse and of guarantees of confidentiality and anonymity. The very nature of the setting, however, has implications for the issue of informed consent. Prisons and hostels are rule-governed institutions which expect individuals to act in particular ways. It remains an unanswered question as to whether women felt they were expected to co-operate with the research, particularly interviews, even though we stressed our independence as researchers and gave them the right to refuse. Moreover, these institutions are semi-public places: places of work as well as temporary homes. Whilst some of these women (although not many) refused to be interviewed, it was difficult for them not to be involved with the observational stages of the research if only in a minor ways.

For those interviewed, the need to obtain their consent as far as possible was crucial but whilst they consented to talk to us, in as much detail as they felt appropriate, it remains questionable how far the consent given was 'informed'. For example, some of the women prisoners and hostel residents were quick to agree to participate before they had listened to a full explanation about the research. Some had mental health problems and others learning difficulties. Others still were foreign nationals not fluent in English and we were not able to provide interpreters. Some were suffering from the side-effects of prescribed medication and/or illegal substances and found it difficult to concentrate. There are other key issues too. Many women in prison and bail hostels are desperate to talk to someone, anyone, who is willing to listen. Other women may (wrongly) feel that something will change as a consequence of their participation and whilst we hoped our research would have positive outcomes, we could not guarantee this.

Securing informed consent when conducting ethnographic observation is notoriously problematic. As Hammersley and Atkinson (1992:265) note 'ethnographers rarely tell *all* the people they are studying *everything* about the research'. However, this does create some ethical tensions. For instance, are people aware that everything they say or do could be used as data? Spending periods of time with participants in an informal way provided us with rich and detailed 'private' accounts, but raises a number of questions about research roles: how did the women view us? Did they see us as researchers or friends and given our feminist approach, what roles were we trying to play?

Fieldwork relationships: researcher, friend or sister?

For both of us, the rejection of distance and objectivity in the researcher-researched relationship which feminists have advocated was influential. Harding (1987) argues that placing the researcher on the same critical plane as her/his research subjects breaks down the false distinction between the 'subject' and 'object' in research. Predominantly concerned with the use of interviews, some feminists have argued that we must strive for non-hierarchical research relationships which are potentially empowering (Oakley, 1981). Whilst such accounts are now often regarded as simplistic and idealistic, the principle of sharing research space is central to feminist methodology (Puwar, 1997).

We quickly discovered that our experiences did not meet this feminist ideal. Establishing rapport and empathy was not inevitable just because we were female researchers researching women and, while in many cases we were able to consciously use various techniques to develop rapport, a sense of 'shared sisterhood' was not an inevitability. The problematic and complex nature of power in feminist research relationships has been debated greatly (Maynard and Purvis, 1994; Patai, 1991; Stacey, 1988). Whilst this is a crucial issue, for us the ethics of research relationships was also a key concern. In particular, to what extent does the search for empathic and close research relationships contribute to a deeper form of exploitation than in the traditional positivistic approaches which feminist have so often rejected?

Stacey (1988:23) has explored these issues in relation to ethnographic research. She argues that 'elements of inequality, exploitation, and even betrayal are endemic to ethnography'. This is an important piece of work, but we would argue that the situation is more complex than Stacey suggests. From the design stages onwards, we hoped we had chosen methods that were compatible with feminist principles. In particular, it was our intention to provide a space in which women could voice their experiences and to some extent set their own agenda. However, one outcome of allowing respondents to choose the depth of their disclosures was that some felt greater distress than they might have done in a more structured interview situation. It was not uncommon for both hostel residents and prisoners, to become distressed when discussing certain topics, particularly those relating to their children and families. This then raises questions about who takes responsibility for the effects of asking respondents to probe painful experiences and emotions (Finch, 1984; Kirkwood, 1993). Ultimately, this responsibility must rest with the researcher. In our attempts to overcome some of these issues, we made time at the end of interviews to 'debrief' respondents and to give recognition to the value of their memories and emotions. While most participants said they had enjoyed the chance to talk to someone in detail, some acknowledged that they had unleashed memories and emotions more powerful and distressing than they had anticipated.

Throughout the fieldwork, we each became very aware of the fine line between enabling respondents to speak in detail about their experiences, and unintentionally steering respondents to experience painful and potentially damaging feelings. We tried to convince ourselves of the benefits of the research. The interviews may have been empowering, providing an opportunity for women to articulate their experiences in the hope that it would lead to change, or they may have been cathartic, providing an outlet for individuals to off-load. More simply, they may have provided women with an opportunity to talk about their experiences to another interested individual. However, awareness of these benefits had to be reconciled with real fears, that we in some unintentional way had caused harm. Were we contributing towards the difficulties already experienced by vulnerable and marginalised women? Here, Glesne and Peshkin's (1992: 112) reflections resonate clearly with our own concerns.

> Questions of exploitation, or 'using' your others, tend to arise as you become immersed in research and begin to rejoice in the richness of what you are learning. You are thankful, but instead of simply appreciating the gift, you may feel guilty for how much you are receiving and how little you are giving in return.

The difficulty here is that the emotional effects of the research can be great (for both the researcher and the researched). Moreover, researchers need to be conscious of their limitations and avoid taking on roles as counsellor or therapist (although this is not to suggest that such services should not be available). This is a crucial ethical dilemma which we could have responded to in a number of ways. We might have abandoned our projects in order to protect the interests of participants. However, not only would this go against our own interests (primarily to obtain Ph.D.s), it would also lead to research being abandoned which could be potentially beneficial, perhaps not directly for the particular women involved but for women who appear before the courts generally. Instead, we continued with our research, reflecting upon the ways in which we tried to ensure the research was as ethical as possible. For example, as Hammersley (1992) argues, our participants did have choices: to agree to take part and to answer questions. However, as we have already noted, for the women prisoners and hostel residents, choices about participation can appear very limited. As feminist researchers, we can try to give something back by, for example, answering questions. However, reciprocation is easier in some relationships than others. Often, women would ask questions which we simply could not answer: What sentence will I receive? What will happen to my children? We were conscious of our limitations and avoided the temptation to try to answer these questions and give reassurances which one might give to a friend.

At another level, there were several occasions in both our projects where ethical problems directly arose as a consequence of our research relationships and what we learned about our respondents. We promised people anonymity and confidentiality and let them know that we could be trusted not to report back. However, throughout the fieldwork we both witnessed first hand, and were told anecdotally, about many aspects of institutional life that posed particular moral dilemmas for us in terms of what we *should* do with the information. We saw instances of staff misconduct (particularly in the prison context) and were both confronted with accounts from women prisoners and hostel residents about incidents of illicit behaviour either resulting in actual harm or with the potential to cause harm to either our respondents themselves or to others. Examples include needle-sharing amongst intravenous drug users, self-harmful ideations and the whereabouts of fragments of glass for persistent 'cutters'. Such knowledge made us feel uncomfortable not least about ourselves. Confidentiality within the context of research in criminal justice institutions can be problematic (see Scraton et al., 1991). However, throughout our researches, confidentiality and anonymity were assured and maintained for each respondent, although we often questioned whether we had done 'the right thing' and, at the end of the day, where would we have drawn the line?

Leaving the field and the consequences of the academic endeavour

Fieldwork raises serious questions about one's personal integrity not least because of the relationships one develops whilst in the field but also because of the possible consequences of the work and ethical commitments continue throughout the research process, even after leaving the field. Kelly (1988), for example, has pointed to the problems involved in transposing the spoken to the written word and Olesen (1995) suggests that a major future question of feminist qualitative research will be the degree to which the various approaches contribute to a sociology *for* rather than *on* women.

Our final texts, presented as our doctoral theses, were structured by ourselves, offering our own interpretations and analysis. The collaborative models propounded by Duelli Klein (1983) and Mies (1983) were not wholly appropriate because of the difficulties of following-up respondents. However, at the end of interviews we asked respondents if there were any other topic areas which they felt were important that should be explored with other study participants. Their recommendations were important in helping us to identify our own assumptions and misunderstandings. Participants also provided valuable suggestions for ways of approaching often sensitive subjects. Also, as core themes were identified they were fed back informally to staff and women prisoners and residents and their assessments of the validity of the data and our interpretations were elicited. Here, frequent visits to our research establishments provided the opportunity to further clarify interpretations and measure their resonance against the experiences of others.

At the writing-up stage, a number of strategies were employed to establish the texts as a sociology for women. For instance, we used the same language which the women themselves used to describe their lives and included their voices through the quotations that peppered the pages of our theses. Such strategies are not, however, unproblematic and a number of difficulties arise when drawing conclusions, interpretations and findings from people's narratives. Offering short 'snippets' may, for example, fragment or even distort, individual experiences (Atkinson, 1992). While we tried not to lose sight of the accounts provided, the interpretation of their stories was ours. In addition, our mode of representation reflects the main purpose of the research, principally to obtain a Ph.D and here we were governed by academic protocol. It may well be that, in order to share the findings with participants or a wider public audience, alternative literary forms are appropriate such as auto-biographical accounts (Ward, 1993; Maguire, 1994), scripts to be performed (Ellis and Bochner, 1992; Mienczakowski, 1996) or poetry (Richardson, 1992).

What is clear to us is that ethical issues continue beyond the period of data collection. Furthermore, once the research has been written up ethical dilemmas remain. Given the sensitivity of much criminological research and the dominance of a law and order stance in current criminal justice policy, there is a danger that research findings can be used in ways that are not expected, for example in justifying the introduction of repressive legislation, and which are far removed from the initial aims of the research.

As doctoral research rather than funded research commissioned by official agencies such as the Home Office, it is difficult to judge the impact (if any) of our researches. Whilst both studies have clear policy implications, they were primarily constructed as projects which would contribute to academic knowledge in general, and feminist criminological scholarship in particular. Kimmel (1988) proposes three strategies to ensure ethical conduct when working in applied settings. First, the researcher needs to predict how the findings will be used. Secondly, they need to be disseminated to a wide audience to reduce the likelihood of a powerful group using them for its own ends. Finally, the researcher should be alert to over hasty conclusions. The latter two strategies are easier to adopt than the former, although the struggle to acquire academic accreditation (through publications) means that certain compromises may be made. It is much more difficult to predict how findings can be used. For example, could critical comments about bail hostel provision for women be used to justify the closure of some bail hostels (under threat at the time of the research) or the escalating female remand population? Could the documentation of women's coping strategies, within prisons and hostels, such as substance use (illegal drugs, alcohol, prescribed medication, food) and self-harm contribute to the medicalisation of women who offend? Hence, whilst we hoped that the research would be beneficial for women in criminal justice institutions and therefore give something back to the participants, this is an aspiration rather than an inevitability.

Some final reflections

This joint reflective account is testimony to the benefits of hindsight, highlighting what we consider to be the main ethical dilemmas encountered in our doctoral researches (there are more!). We believe that our methodological and theoretical approach, coupled with our focus on criminal justice institutions fundamentally shaped the nature of the research process and the ethical issues that confronted us. By reflecting on some of these issues and the interpersonal strategies we adopted during field access negotiations and fieldwork we hope to have highlighted some of the situation-specific problems of qualitative research.

In both pieces of work we experienced tensions in what we assumed to be a feminist methodological approach and the effects of attachments to feminist ideas about the process and practice of research. There may well be a mis-match between the theoretical framework in which the research is located and the *doing* of the research. There are no textbook situations of social reality, however, there remains an assumption that researchers in training should take ethical dilemmas in their stride.

This discussion has implications for the support and supervision of novice researchers who should be encouraged to reflect on the ethical and moral dimensions of their work. Sensitive reflections on the ways in which particular researchers in particular social contexts attempt to manage ethical considerations, whilst no doubt idiosyncratic, are nonetheless valuable not only in terms of minimising the emotional impact of fieldwork (by highlighting that experiences are not unique even if the research is) but also in terms of adding depth to the end product. Here, reflective accounts have a number of general benefits. First, attending to ethical questions in the field is a method of finding out where the researcher stands in relation to those being studied. Secondly, an exploration of the ethics of the relationship between researcher and respondent firmly locates the researcher within the research process. This also allows a discussion of how that process affects the researcher (a neglected issue). Finally, viewing ethnographic research and the Ph.D. experience in general as an ethically charged enterprise opens up the discussion to broader questions of the academic mode of production.

References

Atkinson, P. (1992) *Understanding Ethnographic Texts*, Newbury Park, Ca.: Sage.

Cohen, S. and Taylor, L. (1972) *Psychological Survival: The Experience of Long Term Imprisonment*, Harmondsworth: Penguin.

Duelli Klein, R. (1983) 'Passionate scholarship: notes on values, knowing and methods in feminist social sciences', in G. Bowles and R. Duelli Klein (eds.) *Theories of Women's Studies*, London: Routledge and Kegan Paul.

Ellis, C. and Bochner, A. (1992) 'Telling and performing personal stories: the constraints of choice in abortion', in C. Ellis and G. Flaherty (eds.) *Investigating Subjectivity: Research on Lived Experience*, Newbury Park, Ca.: Sage.

Finch, J. (1984) 'It's great to have someone to talk to: the ethics and politics of interviewing women', in C. Bell and H. Roberts (eds.) *Social Researching*, London: Routledge and Kegan Paul.

Glesne, C. and Peshkin, A. (1992) *Becoming Qualitative Researchers*, White Plains, NY.: Longman.

Hammersley, M. (1992) *What's Wrong with Ethnography?* London: Routledge.

Hammersley, M. and Atkinson, P. (1995) (2nd edition) *Ethnography: Principles in Practice*, London: Routledge.

Harding, S. (1987) (ed.) *Feminism and Methodology*, Milton Keynes: Open University Press.

Howe, A. (1994) *Punish and Critique.* London: Routledge.

Kelly, L. (1990) 'Journeying in reverse: possibilities and problems in feminist research on sexual violence', in L. Gelsthorpe and A. Morris (eds.) *Feminist Perspectives in Criminology*, Milton Keynes: Open University Press.

Kimmel, A. (1988) *Ethics and Values in Applied Social Research*, Newbury Park, Ca.: Sage.

Kirkwood, C. (1993) *Leaving Abusive Partners*, London: Sage.

Liebling, A. (1992) *Suicides in Prison*, London: Routledge.

Maguire, A. (1994) *Why me?* London: Harper Collins.

May, T. (1993) *Social Research: Issues, Methods and Processes.* Milton Keynes: Open University Press.

Maynard, M. and Purvis, J.(1994) (eds.) *Researching Women's Lives from a Feminist Perspective*, London: Taylor and Francis.

Mienczakowski, J. (1996) *An Ethnographic Act: The Construction of Consensual Theatre and the Representation of Research Results*, Paper presented to the 4th International Conference on Social Science Methodology (1996), Unpublished.

Mies, M. (1983) 'Towards a methodology for feminist research', in G. Bowles and R. Duelli Klein (eds.) *Theories of Women's Studies*, London: Routledge and Kegan Paul.

Norris, C. (1993) 'Some Ethical Considerations on Field-Work with the Police' in D. Hobbs and T. May (eds.) *Interpreting the field.* Oxford: Clarendon.

Oakley, A. (1981) 'Interviewing women: a contradiction in terms', In H. Roberts (ed.) *Doing Feminist Research*, London: Routledge.

Olesen, V. (1995) 'Feminisms and models of qualitative research', in Denzin, N. and Lincoln, Y. (eds.) *The Handbook of Qualitative Research,* Newbury Park, Ca.: Sage.

Patai, D. (1991) 'US academics and the third world women: is ethical research possible?, in S. Gluck and D. Patai (eds.) *Women's Words: The Feminist Practice of Oral History*, New York: Routledge.

Puwar, N. (1997) 'Reflections on interviewing women MPs', *Sociological Research Online*, 2: no. 1.

Rice, M. (1990) 'Challenging orthodoxies in feminist theory: a black feminist critique', in L. Gelsthorpe and A. Morris (eds.) *Feminist Perspectives in Criminology*, Milton Keynes: Open University Press.

Richardson, L (1992) 'The consequences of poetic representation: writing the other, writing the self', in C. Ellis and G. Flaherty (eds.) *Investigating Subjectivity: Research on Lived Experience*, Newbury Park, Ca.: Sage.

Scraton, P., Sim, J. and Skidmore, P. (1991) *Prisons Under Protest.* Milton Keynes: Open University Press.

Smart, C. (1976) *Women, Crime and Criminology: A Feminist Critique,* London: Routledge and Kegan Paul.

Smart, C. (1990) 'Feminist approaches to criminology or postmodern woman meets atavistic man', in L. Gelsthorpe and A. Morris (eds.) *Feminist Perspectives in Criminology*, Milton Keynes: Open University Press.

Smartt, U. (1995) *Remand Prisons in England and Germany*, Paper presented at the British Criminology Conference (1995), Unpublished.

Smith, C. (1996) *The Imprisoned Body: Women, Health and Imprisonment*, Unpublished PhD thesis, University of Wales, Bangor.

Smith, C. and Wincup, E (forthcoming) 'Breaking in: Researching women in criminal justice institutions' in R.D. King and E. Wincup (eds) *Doing Research on Crime and Justice*. Oxford: Clarendon Press.

Stacey, J. (1988) 'Can there be a feminist ethnography?', *Women's Studies International Quarterly*, 11: 21-27.

Ward, J. (1993) *Ambushed*. London: Vermilion.

Wincup, E. (1997) *Waiting for Trial: Living and Working in a Bail Hostel*, Unpublished PhD thesis, University of Wales, Cardiff.

9 Privacies and private: making ethical dilemmas public when researching sexuality in the primary school

EMMA RENOLD

Introduction

Discussions surrounding the ethics of conducting research with children have often centred on the issue of informed consent and the problematics of whether children are competent to be able to choose freely and, more specifically if that consent is exercised in a situation of voluntary choice (Thorne, 1993). Despite the UN Convention on the Rights of the Child and the Children Act 1989 (which recognises the wishes, views and experiences of the child), children are still viewed as the property of their parental gate-keepers:

> In the UK, consent is usually taken to mean consent form parents or those in 'loco-parentis', and in this respect children are to a large extent seen as their parents property, devoid of the right to say no to research.
> (Morrow and Richards, 1996:94).

In an article that specifically details the ethical dilemmas involved in social research with children Morrow and Richards (1996) show that neither the British Psychological Society (BPS), British Sociological Association (BSA) or the Association of Social Anthropologists (ASA) have detailed ethical guidelines on conducting research with children as research subjects. The BPS consider children alongside 'adults with impairments' and the ASA and BSA make no specific mention of children. The BSA *Statement of Ethical Practice* however, does stress that 'special care' (whatever that may entail) should be taken with research subjects who are vulnerable by factors of 'age, social status and powerlessness', of which children come under all three criteria (Morrow and Richards, 1996:93).

However, with the expansion of sociological research into the neglected area of children and childhoods in which children are no longer viewed through developmental concepts which locate them as 'immature' and 'passive by-standers' within processes of socialisation, a concomitant shift within a growing body of research has similarly re-examined children's involvement in the research process (Qvortrup, 1994; Mayall, 1994; Butler and Shaw, 1995; Alderson, 1995; James and Prout, 1998). Within the 'new' sociology of children and childhood, children are perceived as active, constructive and value producing and worthy of study in their own right. From the 'object' to the 'subject' of research, children are no longer researched 'on' but 'with' and their accounts of social reality and personal experience are taken as competent portrayals of their experiences.

Such 'participatory research' (Hill, 1997) has broadened discussions on ethical practice when researching children to encompass not only issues around ensuring that children are given the opportunity not to participate, ('informed dissent') and maintaining or renewing that consent. But researchers are also enabling children to have more control over what they are consenting to by finding ways and developing methods in which children themselves can set the agenda of the research. However, conducting research in this way by enabling children to have some control over its focus can raise its own ethical issues and dilemmas, especially when the focus of that research develops and changes, and taps into previously unexplored, unexpected and sensitive territory. The aim of this chapter is to outline and explore some of those issues and dilemmas, how they were experienced at the time and how they were resolved.

I have divided the chapter into four sections. Firstly I will give an overview of the research topic and then move on to describe the processes and negotiations involved in accessing children's worlds, before moving on to map out the methodological aims which led to the re-focusing of the research. The 'unexpected tales' and subsequent ethical dilemmas that arose from this redirection are presented in the style of the 'confessional' and further analysed in the final section.

Background to the study: from gender to sexuality

The data presented in this paper derive from recently completed doctoral research exploring the salience of gender and sexuality through the accounts by, and observations of, boys and girls in their last year of primary school (see Renold, 1999). The research took place within two primary schools located in a small town in the East of England over a period of one year. With little existing UK research into how children perceive and construct their gendered identities, I initially (Summer 1994) conducted a six week pilot study in two year 6 classrooms, with a view to identifying what it means to occupy and live out the categories 'girl' and 'boy' at school using an ethnographic concoction of detailed participant observations, in-depth unstructured exploratory group interviews and focus groups. And, as in many ethnographic studies, the flexibility and reflexivity of the ethnographic process led to a shift in focus and the inevitable 'Pandora's box' indicative of qualitative research. During the first term of the academic year I was increasingly witnessing the complex daily interactive network of heterosexual performances by both girls and boys as they negotiated their gendered selves. And by adopting methods that harnessed the 'children's standpoint' (Alanen, 1994), in which children could exercise some control over the focus of the research, previously unreported and private accounts of children's sexual cultures, described by Best (1983) as the 'third hidden curriculum', began to surface. From examining gender relations I found myself also examining sexual relations and the formation of sexual identities. The following section breaks down how an adult researcher accessed the more private domain of children's worlds and then goes on to discuss the ethical dilemmas, both personal and political which ensued when such private disclosures were made public.

Accessing children's worlds

Physicality

Like Thorne, many researchers involved in studying children have to deal with or overturn conventional adult-child relationships. As Corsaro (1981) notes, when nicknamed 'Big Bill' on 'entering the child's world', one of these differences is that of size and adult physical characteristics. Glassner, in his discussion also stresses that the researcher is physically unable to pass unnoticed in the company of children (Fine and Glassner, 1979). However, where these and other researcher felt too big or too old, with physical characteristics that matched only other adults and not other children, my differences were less pronounced, less obvious. Girls and boys would walk up to me and compare heights (many of them were taller). Thus, my height did not visibly mark me as 'different'. I also talked much the same as them, with a similar accent and pitch. My age, although 22/23, was often overlooked by the pupils, many of whom initially presumed (although I was honest about my age), that I was a visiting Year 10/11 from the local comprehensive. Dress was also a feature that *included* me in their 'cultures' rather than positioning me outside it. It was my status as *researcher* (see also Hill et al,. 1996; Mauther, 1996; Alldred, 1998; Graue and Walsh, 1998), as authoritative 'adult' and the power embedded within these identities that was constantly negotiated on accessing children's worlds.

Authority

To overcome some of the boundaries of authority I insisted to be called by my first name and as far as possible declined teaching scenarios that would position me as knowledgeable and intellectually superior. Similarly, on the playground I did not stand with the dinner ladies so as to mark myself off from possessing formal authoritative powers. The majority of my time was spent with other children, away from the staffroom and visible contact with their class teacher or other staff. Adopting a less adult-centric stance came with regular testing of my authoritative boundaries. Openly swearing, fighting, passing notes, giggling and making faces behind teacher's backs was not uncommon during the early stages of fieldwork.

Committed to the idea of 'least adult role' (Mandell, 1988), like Corsaro (1981) in his study of infant children, when observing in the playground and classroom, I would also wait until children approached me or invited me to join in or listen to their conversations. Being 'reactive' rather than initiating reactions went some way to equalising the inter-generational dynamics in the adult/child relationship (Corsaro, 1997). It also allowed children more control over their participation in the research process. As discussed in the introduction this also included the right not to participate in the research.

Learning and listening

Thorne (1993:14) explains that 'to learn from children, adults have to challenge the deep assumption that they already know what children are 'like', both because, as former children, adults have been there, and because, as adults, they regard children as less complete versions than themselves'. Similarly, learning from children, rendering their worlds strange and not assuming that their social meanings and interpretations to events, experiences and language are our social meanings (Fine and Glassner, 1979:170), I spent a great deal of time asking them to explain what they meant by certain words or phrases. This also went some way to reinforcing my positioning of non-authoritative adult. Similarly, listening was an integral part of the research process. This included listening to boys' and girls' problems that often positioned me as 'agony aunt', as interviews, both recorded and unrecorded, sometimes turned into 'therapy' sessions (Brannen, 1988; Hemmings and Cocklin, 1997). What was important was not just listening to their stories, but taking them seriously and not trivialising their accounts. Over time, this brought more of their (often silenced) voices from the margins and facilitated the environment for the more 'unexpected tales'.

Negotiating trust and issues of confidentiality

Trying to overcome some of the problems embedded in the adult/child binary by sharing, listening, watching, learning and collaborating in the least adult-centric way, helped develop trusting relationships between myself and the research participants. But as Fine and Glassner (1979:167) note, 'any intimate sharing relationship will take time to develop and may never be pressured'. Thus, waiting and avoiding pressuring or probing insensitively was fundamental to gaining children's trust. For example, even though I knew of its existence, it took six months for a group of boys to disclose to me the chronic bullying they had received from others in the class.

Reflexivity was also fundamental in establishing trusting relationships (Mauthner, 1996). One boy, when I had asked him personal questions about his friends, interests, hobbies and family grabbed my note book and said, 'right now it's your turn' and asked me the same questions. Establishing trust also extended to other children not directly involved in the research. In fact, I became more conscious that I had gained their trust when I witnessed a group of boys and girls aggressively talking (and swearing) about who had broken the toilet window. One of the girls from another class spotted me and nudged the others to stop talking. However, a boy from the class I *was* researching said, 'no she's all right, she won't tell', and they continued their discussion. Not 'telling' was vital in ensuring confidentiality. Yet despite informing them from the beginning of the research, that everything I witnessed or that they disclosed to me would not be shown to anybody, pupil or teacher, it needed repeating on a regular basis. Establishing children's trust was a long and reflexive series of negotiations.

Empowerment, voice and the children's standpoint

One of the central features of the research was its commitment to foregrounding children's own experiences and allowing them to wield some control over the focus of the research. Alanen (1994) has described this approach as research conducted from the 'children's standpoint', that is giving voice and respecting children as knowledgeable and active subjects. Part of this approach involves using the research process as a platform, which can enable children to communicate experiences of importance to them. It also involves adopting a reciprocal and reflexive relationship between the researcher and researched thus 'giving voice' and 'hearing the voices' of children and rendering them as 'deserving and capable of articulating their perspectives' (Alldred, 1998:160).

In relation to my own research, the decision to utilise exploratory unstructured group interviews as one of the predominant ethnographic methods was founded on children's ability to create spaces (both within their discursive and physical location, conducted away from teachers and other staff members) from which they could freely discuss what they felt to be important to them. My role, during these 'interviews' was more of a facilitator, where once conversations had started I would interject at specific moments to probe and encourage children to develop some of the things they had said. To this end I would refrain from asking questions and as far as possible allow the children themselves to set the agenda for the topic of discussion. Moreover, by interviewing repeatedly over the year, it was possible to develop with most of the children in the study (some more than others) a safe, comfortable and supportive relationship/environment with which they could discuss, disclose and share their experiences. What I had not anticipated were the more private disclosures of their more intimate sexual worlds and relations which the above approach and my unique relationship to them seemed to have facilitated. To offer some insight into a researcher's exposure to and feelings towards some unexpected 'data' and the ensuing ethical issues and dilemmas that arose, I have re-constructed the fieldnotes, interview extracts and emotions of my first 'sensitive moments'.

Some unexpected tales

In their chapter on ethics and ethnography, Hammersley and Atkinson (1995) stress that at the initial point of negotiating access, the ethnnographer herself does not know the course the work will take. Utilising a methodology which enabled children to use many of our interviews as forums to discuss what was of significance to them, combined with the development of mutual trust and my commitment to confidentiality, many of the children allowed me access to their more private thoughts, experiences and relationships. I had been prepared for access to the more public knowledge and rituals of the playground that surrounded the discourses and practices of boyfriend and girlfriend relationships. I had also expected, as a female researcher, possible access to the often secret domain of girls' friendships networks as previous researchers have explored (Hey, 1997; Griffiths, 1997; Davies, 1993; McRobbie, 1991; Lees, 1993). Previous literature on female researchers accessing 'boyhood' and male adolescent cultures, however, had all suggested that these kinds of tales would remain private, untold and unseen (Best, 1983; Askew and Ross, 1988). Thus, I had not anticipated entry to boys' more private worlds and as the following extract portrays, their sexual practices and fantasies.

Context

The following extract is taken from an interview in which boys were talking about the toys they had played with when they were younger. They then go on to discuss the games they used to play when they were eight and nine.

The first column displays the fieldnotes taken at the time of the interview and expanded later that evening. The second column re-creates my thoughts and emotions from the interview (with the aid of my personal journal).

Expanded fieldnotes	**Private thoughts and emotions**
Toby and Steven tell me that some of their favourite games when they were in Year 4 (age 9) were fantasy games and they still play them today.	*This is an area I am particularly interested in, knowing that this group still play fantasy games on the playground, when all the other boys are playing football.*
I ask them what did they used to play when they were younger. Steven replies:	
'Well we used to play one game where we were in my bedroom and we made a van out of stuff. We used to pretend that we broke into the school using the van and drove into the playground to kidnap the girls we used to fancy at the time ... after we got them into the van we pretended to have it off with them on the bed'.	*As the story progresses, I am scribbling down Steven's story almost word for word. I can't believe that they are sharing something so personal with me. I assumed that, now a couple of years older, they would find the games they played when they were younger as embarrassing, as other boys (and girls) have done. But, they are all listening to Steven and no one is giggling or sniggering.*
Steven then continues to describe that they used to act 'having it off' with each other. One of them would pretend to be the girl and one the kidnapper.	*What does this mean? my mind is working overtime as I unravel the possible hetero- and homosexual relations involved in their game and the fact that they are disclosing this in front of me.*
At this point, Simon interjects with 'so did I' and informs the group that he and his best friend used to play the same game. Now they all fall about laughing.	*If these are common experiences then that could explain why the others were not making fun of Steven.*
They then go on to describe the girls they used to fancy.	
Meanwhile, Aaron is talking to Ben about how when people talk about sex, it gives him an erection. Ben laughs.	*On hearing this I find myself avoiding eye contact with Aaron and begin my note-taking again. I find myself becoming increasingly aware of the nature and focus of the discussion and wonder how a discussion on toys and games has developed into an exploration of sexuality and sexual knowledge.*

[I hear a noise at the entrance to the classroom we are interviewing in. I look around, but there is no-one there - the boys continue to talk, they almost seem to have forgotten I am here]	*The noise at the door and the possibility of eave-droppers makes me re-assess the situation and I begin imagining all kinds of sensationalist media headlines. I also begin to imagine the head-teacher's response in my allowing the boys to discuss something so intimate.*
	I continue to listen and make a mental note to re-think the ethical issue of 'informed consent'.
Toby hears Aaron talk about erections and starts laughing and then quite seriously begins to describe how his penis enlarges. Simon then exclaims, almost in amazement, how penises in general can go from being so small to something so big.	*Their frank and sincere discussion about their maturing bodies and sexual awareness amazes me.*
	Should I change the subject? How would they react if I did? Why do I want to change the subject?
Toby laughs and shows the transformation in size of his own penis. At this point, the bell rings and we disperse as pupils start lining up outside the classroom. Collecting my things together, I begin to ponder on the experiences that have just been shared.	*Saved by the bell, this time, but I need to reflect more on the ethical issues of 'collecting data' on the sexual lives and experiences of children in a study that was initially examining 'gender relations'.*

Imaginary fears and moral panics

On engaging in research with children, Graue and Walsh (1998:60) warn that being in the field will at times make one uncomfortable because children may 'tell me things I don't want to hear and show me things I don't want to see'. Indeed, some researchers may have found the boys' frank discussion surrounding their sexual knowledge and practices disturbing, thus creating feelings of discomfort. However, my concerns regarding the disclosures were not regarding my own personal fears and worries about the nature or content of the boys' talk. My anxieties lay in the imaginary fears and moral panics of others. Realising the sensitivity involved in conflating children or childhood with sexuality, I found myself imagining sensationalist media headlines. What if? questions during and after the interview bombarded my thoughts as I created scenarios of the boys telling their mums, dads and grand-parents what they had 'learnt at school today', even though I knew that sharing such personal information with their parents would be anathema to them.

Informed consent?

My next concern involved the informed consent of 'gatekeepers' to the research and the fear of our conversations being overheard or leaked into the public domain. Although my initial description of the research was loosely phrased as 'exploring what it means to be a boy and a girl at school from the child's perspective', I suspect that the teachers and head teachers were not aware that exploring gender could also involve exploring sexuality; although they were aware that I was exploring children's social networks which included boyfriends and girlfriends. In my favour, I had stressed that our interviews and 'chats' would remain confidential unless they or others were at serious risk or harm. However, parents were only informed of the research through the schools' newsletter, and it could be questioned whether they were *fully* informed of the research and its focus. Consequently, making the decision to continue to enable children the freedom to share their more private experiences could involve the risk of exposure and possible termination of access to the focus schools.

However, I was also very conscious of tapping into previous unreported sexual subjectivities regarding boys' sexual cultures and decided on further reflection that a trade-off, albeit risky, needed to be made between the 'data' generated from the children, as research participants, and the gatekeepers to the research site. This decision was also informed by the possibility that terminating, censoring or steering conversations which took a 'sexual' turn would have a negative affect on both boys and girls' understandings of sexuality and sexual practices. It could also damage the open and trusting relationship that had developed over the preceding months, which could, in turn prevent intimate disclosures of a different nature. Moreover, such action would contradict and contravene my methodological decision to conduct research from the children's standpoint. These issues are discussed further below.

Maintaining the children's standpoint

Myths surrounding the sexualisation/de-sexualisation of children to promote discourses of childhood innocence are prevalent, hence the dearth of current and past research into childhood and sexuality (Jackson, 1982; Thorne and Luria, 1986) that covers more than sexual abuse or deviance. Corsaro's (1997:302) landmark text, 'The Sociology of Childhood' for example, has no reference to 'sexuality', only 'sexual orientation' and this is located in the index after 'sexual molestation' and before 'peer abuse'. The following two quotes encapsulate society's ambiguous attitude to children's sexuality and informed my decision not to intervene or re-focus conversations in which children (boys in this case) chose to share the sexual side of their childhoods.

They [children] are assumed to lack sexual curiosity, knowledge or beliefs: they ought to be wholly unconscious of 'such things' - should not even be beginning to think about understanding them, never mind understanding them (Epstein and Johnson, 1998:96).

They know and probably do too much, too soon, too young. Sexually they are not childish enough (Epstein and Johnson, 1998:36).

Only too aware of how society suppresses childhood sexuality and how childhood innocence is something which adults wish upon young children and thus not a 'natural' feature of childhood itself, my initial fears surrounding the 'informed consent' of adult gatekeepers and my reactionary imaginary moral panics were soon allayed as I was increasingly privy to the 'third hidden curriculum' of children's sexual cultures. As the year progressed, and with my commitment to foregrounding children's views and focusing the research from their standpoint, I was gathering 'data' that could refute the claims above and create new discursive spaces about how children forge their sexual identities and relations. It was thus possible to begin exploding the myth of de-sexualised and sanitised childhoods and explore how girls and boys regularly move in and out of official 'innocent' childhood discourses and in and out of discourses of overt sexuality and sexual practices. I was also sensitive of conveying and reinforcing messages of sexuality as shameful or taboo had I changed the topic of conversation.

Looking back, I may or may not have taken a risk in continuing to hear and listen to children's more intimate and more private experiences. My fears may have remained unfounded. However, by not foreclosing areas deemed socially taboo, children continued to share their experiences with me over the year. Some of these experiences were of a similar nature to the scenarios presented in this chapter. Other disclosures included sexual physical harassment, homophobic bullying and abuse and more general insecurities regarding current and future heterosexual relationships. All, however, were topics that the children, as participants, defined and re-defined for themselves and thus went some way to equalising the inter-generational dynamics of adult researcher, child-participant and changing how we come to conduct and involve research with children.

Conclusion

This chapter has provided a 'confessional' account of the ethical dilemmas that can arise when the focus of the research develops and changes during the course of the study. More specifically I have highlighted how the relationship between the gatekeepers and participants are re-assessed in light of the researcher's methodological rationales, aims and commitments. Re-presenting notes and thoughts from the field, I illustrated how my commitment to carry out research from the 'children's standpoint' which involves children themselves to set the focus for debate and discussion, can lead the researcher into unexpected and uncharted territories, which in this case, involved the more sensitive and controversial domain of children's sexual cultures. To maintain the trust developed between the researcher and particpants, to ensure confidentiality and to continue to hear similar disclosures and experiences, a methodological decision was taken not to re-negotiate the new focus of the research with the 'adult' gatekeepers. There are, of course, further ethical considerations regarding interpretation and publication when accessing and collecting sensitive 'data' in this way and issues around what it means as a young female researcher to explore boys' sexuality and sexual practices. These are, however, 'tales' for another paper. The purpose of this paper is to contribute to the growing number of accounts in which ethical issues are discussed openly and publicly so that they can feed directly into the discussions and deliberations of future research.

References

Alanen, L. (1994) Gender and Generation: Feminism and the Child Question, in Qvortrup et al. (Eds.) (1994), *Childhood Matters: Social Theory, Practice and Politics.* Aldershot: Avebury Publishing.

Alderson, P. (1995) *Listening to Children*, London: Barnardos.

Alldred, P. (1998) Ethnography and Discourse Analysis: Dilemmas in Representing the Voices of Children, in J. Ribbens and R. Edwards (Eds.) (1998), *Public Knowledge and Private Lives*, London: Sage Publications Ltd.

Askew, S. (1989) Aggressive Behaviour in Boys: To What Extent is it Institutionalised?, in D.P. Tattum and D.A. Lane (Eds.) (1989) *Bullying in Schools*, Stoke on Trent: Trentham Books.

Best, R. (1983) *We've all got scars: What Girls and Boys Learn in Elementary School,* Bloomington: Indiana University Press.

Butler, I. and Shaw, I. (Eds.) (1996) *A Case of Neglect?: Children's Experiences and the Sociology of Childhood*, Aldershot:Avebury.

Brannen, J. (1988) Research Note: The Study of Sensitive Subjects, *Sociological Review*, 36 (3) pp.552-563.

Corsaro, W.A. (1981) Entering the Child's World: Research Strategies for Field Entry and Data Collection in a Pre-school Setting, in J. Green and C. Wallet, *Ethnography and Language in Educational Settings*, U.S.A.: Ablex Publishing Corporation.

Davies, B. (1993) *Shards of Glass: Children Reading and Writing Beyond Gendered Identities*, New Jersey: Hampton Press Inc.

Epstein, D. and Johnson, R. (1998) *Schooling Sexualities*, Buckingham: Open University Press.

Fine, A. and Glassner, B. (1979) Participant Observation with Children: Promise and Problems, *Urban Life*, 8 (2) pp.153-174.

Graue, E.M. and Walsh, D.J. (1998) *Studying Children in Context: Theories, Methods and Ethics*, London: Sage Publications.

Griffiths, V. (1995) *Adolescent Girls and their Friends: A Feminist Ethnography*, Aldershot: Avebury.

Hammersley, M. and Atkinson, P. (1995) (2nd Edition) *Ethnography: Principles in Practice*, London: Routledge.

Hemmings, L. and Cocklin, B. (1997) Feminist Oral History: A Reflective Analysis, Paper Presented at *European Conference for Education Research*, Seville, 25th -28th September, pp.1-14.

Hey, V. (1997) *The Company She Keeps: An Ethnography of Girls' Friendships*, Buckingham: Open University Press.

Hill, M., Laybourn, L. and Borland, M. (1996) Engaging with Primary-aged Children About Their Emotions and Well-being: Methodological Considerations, *Children and Society*, 10, pp.129-144.

Hill, M. (1997a) Research Review: Participatory Research with Children, *Child and Family Social Work*, 2, pp.171-183.

Jackson, S. (1982) *Childhood and Sexuality*, Oxford: Basil Blackwell Ltd.

James, A. and Prout, A. (Eds.) (1998) *Constructing and Reconstructing Childhood: Contemporary Issues in the Sociological Study of Childhood*, London: The Falmer Press.

Lees, S. (1993) *Sugar and Spice: Sexuality and Adolescent Girls*, London: Penguin Books Ltd.

Mandell, N. (1988) The Least-Adult Role in Studying Children, *Contemporary Journal of Contemporary Ethnography*, 16 (4) pp.433-467.

Mauthner, M. (1997) Methodological Aspects of Collecting Data from Children: Lessons from Three Research Projects, *Children and Society*, 11, pp.16-28.

Mayall, B. (Ed.) (1994) *Children's Childhoods: Observed and Experienced*, London: The Falmer Press.

McRobbie, A.(1991) *Feminism and Youth Culture: From 'Jackie' to 'Just Seventeen'*, London: Macmillan.

Morrow, V. and Richards, M. (1996) The Ethics of Social Research with Children: An Overview, *Children and Society*, 10, pp.39-49.

Qvortrup,.J. (1994) Childhood Matters: An Introduction, in J. Qvortrup, M. Brady, G. Sgritto and H. Winterberger (Eds.) (1994) *Childhood Matters: Social Theory, Practice and Politics*, Aldershot: Avebury Publishing.

Renold, E. (1999) Presumed Innocence: An Ethnographic Exploration into the construction of sexual and gender identities in the primary school, Unpublished Dissertation, University of Wales, Cardiff.

Thorne, B. (1993) *Gender Play: Boys and Girls in School*, Buckingham: Open University Press.

Thorne, B. and Luria, Z. (1986) Sexuality and Gender in Children's Daily Worlds, *Social Problems*, 33 (3) pp.176-190.

10 Research and the 'fate of idealism': ethical tales and ethnography in a theological college

TREVOR WELLAND

After the communion service most of the students wandered slowly in small groups to the Student Common Room for tea or coffee. I walked next to Donald and we chatted about teaching liturgy and worship in a secular university setting.....Whilst queuing for coffee, I noticed Lucinda ahead of me and I asked her 'So, how is it all going'? David looked up from pouring himself a cup of tea and, seemingly anxious, warned Lucinda sternly and loudly, 'don't tell him anything, he's researching us!'
Research diary extract

Introduction

Measor and Woods (1991) write of the 'untidy nature' of the research process and of being 'in the field' in qualitative inquiry. In confirmation of this observation, this chapter describes and elucidates the 'hybrid' nature of the realities involved in constructing an 'observer-as participant' role while researching the occupational preparation and socialisation of a group of full-time trainees for ordained ministry. It particularly focuses on the management of ethical issues and dilemmas arising from reciprocity and the inevitable interplay of truth, dissimulation and 'degrees of deceit' (Fine, 1993) that emerged through an intense engagement with the social actors in this research setting. This chapter also explores the ways in which undertaking ethnographic field research for the first time resulted in confronting and deviating from anticipated 'idealistic' ethical principles derived from my readings of professional codes of ethical conduct.

Ethnographic texts are characterised by the personal and personalised dimensions of doing fieldwork. In part this is due to the anthropologist's somewhat 'muscular' and physical assertion that 'fieldwork is learned in and through its doing' (Emerson, 1983:ix). Emerson, Fretz and Shaw (1995:3), for example, write of ethnographic participation as 'consequential presence', and draw on Goffman (1989:125) in reinforcing the idea that field research involves 'subjecting yourself, your own body and your own personality, and your own social situation to the set of contingencies that play upon a set of individuals, so that you can physically and ecologically penetrate their circle of response to their social situation or their work situation'. As Grills (1998:163) has commented, 'because ethnographers are the "research instruments", everything that we are gets thrown into the mix'. In undertaking the research reported here, this was to be especially the case. I was researching a residential-based training setting very familiar to me, since I had trained as a Roman Catholic priest during the mid-late 1980s and had been ordained in 1989. I carried and used this biography in an unsettling cocktail of 'confronting and exorcising demons' through re-appraising my own experiences of life in a theological college, and sociologically analysing the ritual, processes and procedures of occupational preparation at St. David's. My past professional identity was expressed in my familiarity with the language of faith and Theology, and irrevocably written on the self as my body remembered with ease the prayerful grace and flow of liturgical movement and gesture.

I have started with the above research diary extract because it seems to capture, and for me foreshadowed, something of the essence of 'doing' ethnography. The extract, in part, represents the traditional ethnographic challenge. It is incumbent upon the active field researcher to 'get in and get close' (Emerson et al., 1995:1), to establish physical and social proximity and, thereby, create a context within which she/he can elicit information and within which the participants will 'show and tell' a great deal. As such, some accounts of ethnographic enquiry exhort novice researchers to establish a deep sense of rapport and intimacy in order to be able to facilitate an 'emic perspective' and thick descriptions of the setting(s) and participants being researched. Hence, the researcher, to some extent at least, is positioned as a dynamic manager, both of the emerging field process and of the resulting field relationships. Fine (1993:274), for example, writes of the 'grail of informed consent' and the blurred boundaries between informed and uninformed. He points out that informed consent is a goal, and that degrees of deceit are inevitable in 'grounded projects'. The choices we make as researchers are inevitably deceitful and made from positions of power that involve the gatekeeping of information.

In addition, Epstein and Johnson (1997:131) in writing of teaching as a form of 'seduction', provide a useful metaphor for the privileged but self-conscious and highly artful means of gaining access to information on the part of the ethnographer; information that is usually only made available to a confidante or friend. The ethical issues located around these dimensions arise specifically because of the more explicit features of the personal and personal detail in ethnographic work (Mason, 1996). The fluid, situated and context-bound nature of ethnographic fieldwork, then, involves the intimate interweavings of impression management, the construction and disclosure of identities and information and the collection of data. It is suffused with and permeated by power dynamics. As I experienced for myself, for the novice researcher a key challenge was that of how one manages and resolves these ethical problems.

In describing here something of my own responses to these issues, this chapter functions as a 'confessional tale' (Van Maanen, 1988) and firmly locates the writer/researcher within the study and its outcomes. In doing so, I also consciously bear testimony to the fact that reflexivity and reflexive involvement are necessary characteristics of the ethnographic tradition.

Methods

This discussion is grounded with qualitative data from a doctoral project, the field research having been undertaken between September 1996 and March 1998. The research maps and explores the professional socialisation of a group of trainee priests within one theological college. In seeking to render visible and problematic something of the 'choreography' of training for ordained ministry, it was important that I also became a part of what the trainees themselves experienced. I, therefore, decided to adopt an ethnographic approach, using qualitative methods of participant observation and informal, semi-structured interviews, as well as analysis of a range of documentary evidence.

Intense observation was carried out mainly during September-June of the first year of fieldwork. Observation was selected as a main research strategy during my time 'in the field', since I wanted to understand the routine aspects of life in this setting and experience recurring structural, interactional and meaning patterns, as well as to share in the participants' world and activities. During my first days in the field and throughout the early part of the first period of fieldwork, I had no real policy in terms of what I observed or the gathering of data. My primary concern was with establishing rapport with the students and staff. However, throughout the next nine months I undertook observations of the weekly, 'in house'

Pastoral Theology course (Thursdays, 2-5pm) and University-based Lectures on Tuesday afternoons and Thursday mornings. In addition, I would 'linger and loiter' after attending the main evening chapel services, as well as at lunch and evening meal times and on Sunday tea afternoons. Fieldnotes were made throughout this period of observation and expanded accounts based on these initial notes were produced as soon as I was away from the setting.

From January 1997-March 1998, 16 students, two senior staff members and a member of the regulatory Board of Ministry were interviewed. Interviews were conducted face-to-face with participants over a period of one to two hours. As is common with ethnographic interviews, a loosely framed schedule was followed which covered the following key areas: the background to vocation and calling; selection processes; perceptions of skills and qualities necessary for ordained ministry; expectations of training; experiences of the training programme and the assessment of competency. In addition, five female candidates participated in a focus group early in the second year of fieldwork. Interviews and the focus group session were tape-recorded and transcribed.

I also found that a variety of documents were of interest to the research and that a great deal of information could be derived from easily accessible sources such as the college prospectus, noticeboards, student timetables and the diaries which they kept whilst on pastoral placements.

St. David's: introducing the trainees and the course

The fourteen theological colleges in England, Scotland and Wales provide a residential setting for the full-time, vocational training of candidates for stipendiary (salaried) ministry that have been centrally selected and sponsored by the various denominations of the Anglican Communion. All of the major denominational communities (Anglican, Roman Catholic, Methodist) require candidates for ordination to complete some form of basic theological training, and the theological colleges (or seminaries) aim to equip candidates for ordained ministry through the diversity of courses offered. In some ways the theological colleges can be viewed as good examples of 'greedy institutions' (Coser, 1974) in terms of the multiple demands (physical, intellectual and spiritual) made on their trainees. To embark on one of the training courses provided is to begin a period of 'challenging uncertainty' (Davies, 1998) which involves separation from the trainee's ordinary lay status and the adoption of a 'threshold', or 'liminal' status, prior to ordination (Davies, 1998:227-233). In order to attain the social status and identity conferred through the ordination rites, students must voluntarily undergo this 'rite of passage' that prepares them for specific roles and networks of social expectation (Coxon, 1965). The unique function of the theological colleges, therefore, is to facilitate this transition through the transmission of a 'sacred tradition' (Hughes and DeBaggis, 1973:181) that consists of an 'ideological' component (a set of theological doctrines), a moral code and a pastoral role that involves both cultic/ritualised forms, as well as what could be broadly termed 'counselling'. These emphases in training have led to ordained ministry being variously described as a 'humanistic profession' (Kleinman, 1984) or an 'ideological profession' (Curcione, 1971).

The training programmes consist of four major areas of study, including Biblical Studies; History of the Judaeo-Christian Tradition; Theology and 'Professional Studies'. Encountering and exploring these intellectual arenas contributes to the development of and a familiarity with a 'professional language' (Kleinman, 1984) that comes to permeate the speech of the students' everyday interactions. However, whereas in other occupational groups this learned indexicality and acquired 'translation competence' might help lay claim to an exclusive expertise and monopoly of the right to practise it, it has been argued that trainees within the theological colleges are being prepared for an 'ill-defined task' or an 'open ended social role' (Davies, 1998:228) since the churches now operate within social matrices that are more secularised, and ordained ministers have had to adapt by becoming 'humanistic professionals' (Kleinman, 1984) that have adopted social roles and functions associated more with the 'emotional labour' of caring professions, such as social work or counselling.

St. David's College, the setting for this piece of research, was founded early in the 1900s, and is situated in the fashionable area of Bishoptown, a 'leafy' suburb of Westcity. The main buildings of the college are adjacent to the ancient Bishoptown Cathedral and 'symbolic links' were maintained through regular student participation in liturgical services. Such links, as well as the presence of visiting bishops or senior clergy, reinforced the hierarchical nature and context of the ecclesiastical setting within which the trainees would work once ordained. These formal networks of social relations are also functional in the mediation of occupational 'enculturation' and professional 'habitus' (Bourdieu, 1990).

During the first period of fieldwork (September 1996-June 1997), the College was responsible for training twenty full-time, residential students (four women, and sixteen men) in three year groups. As in other ethnographic studies of training settings and among groups of trainees (e.g. Atkinson, 1981; Davies, 1988; Parry, 1988; Coffey, 1993; and Salisbury, 1994) these students were marked by their heterogeneity. Their ages ranged from twenty-four to fifty-five years. There was a high degree of 'spatial specialisation' (Goffman, 1961) within the college since, whilst married couples and 'singles' lived within the same community, the 'singles' lived in small study-bedrooms (similar to those in residential halls on university campuses), whilst couples and families occupied 'family homes' owned by the college, which were on, or close to, the college grounds. In addition, the students had diverse occupational backgrounds, for example teaching, research science, financial, social and police work. Six of the students had entered St. David's two to three years after graduating from university, or completing postgraduate research or degrees.

The college was also served by three, full-time, male members of staff who were all priests. They acted as leaders to student tutorial groups of mixed age, sex, year group and 'churchmanship'. In addition to these, the college also cited in its prospectus the use of a range of part-time staff involved in academic studies at the university, pastoral studies 'in house' and 'Spiritual Directors' who, for a short period each term, were resident in college.

At the beginning of their period of formal training the new trainees experience a one week 'induction course'. During this time they were introduced to the 'College Rule' (the institutional 'manual' for communal living) and the structured routine at the college. In addition, all of the trainees register for their academic courses at a local university. In order to determine which course the students will follow, they are individually interviewed by the theological college staff. The different courses validated and inspected by the national Board of Ministry were designed to match the ability levels, previous educational experiences and proposed length of study of the different students. These academic courses were taught mainly within the Department of Theology at the local University of Westcity, where the St. David's staff members also lectured, and were delivered through a programme of lectures and seminars.

In addition to the formal, academic aspects of training, St. David's arranged certain 'at home' courses with a more skills-based focus. These compulsory courses included 'Pastoral Care in the Parish' which was timetabled on Thursday afternoons. This was designed to introduce students both theoretically and practically to a range of pastoral skills necessary for ordained ministry e.g. the rites and processes involved in preaching and conducting marriages, funerals and baptisms. Students were also linked to local parishes during their period of training and were expected to spend part of each Sunday assisting in the services and preaching twice per term. During the long summer vacation period students would spend up to a month in a parish in their home Diocese (geographical area), as well as gaining experience 'shadowing' chaplains in schools and hospitals.

Trust and deceit: establishing rapport and the problem of 'dirty hands'

The research diary extract quoted at the beginning of this chapter describes something of the feeling of suspicion on the part of some of the trainees when I first started the period of fieldwork. After all, this was overt field research and, for the students at least, I was an uninvited outsider who was obviously being 'sponsored' by members of staff, especially Donald the Deputy Principal. The challenge, then, was to navigate the demands of being both stranger and friend (Carvie, 1982) and to establish trust and good relationships with both staff and students. These degrees of progressive and developing intimacy, as already outlined in the introduction to this chapter, inevitably raised ethical issues and dilemmas. Scrutiny of the professional guidelines on ethics (BSA, 1993) and the work of some other researchers before beginning the fieldwork period cautioned me to:

- respect privacy;
- strive for honesty and openness in the relationships formed;
- guard against the misrepresentation of the setting or individuals within it; and
- take responsibility for protecting future research, or other researchers who might wish to do work after me.

Once initial access had been secured and the fieldwork began, it became obvious that, whilst these issues do not diminish in importance and that negotiating and re-negotiating access throughout the process drew on these guidelines, nothing had prepared me for an inevitable navigation of the 'tensions' generated between these 'abstract' principles and the concrete or material situations that I encountered on a regular basis in the field (Cassell and Jacobs, 1987).

Smith (1990:20) writes that 'ethics has to do with how one treats those with whom one interacts and is involved with, and how the relationships formed may depart from some conception of an ideal.' In beginning to address these dilemmas, I began to realise something of the situational complexity of field work practice (Norris, 1993:125), or what Klockars (1979:265) has called the 'problem of dirty hands'. An example of this was experienced after having interviewed Lucinda, a mature first year student who had decided to protest at, what she perceived to be, the complete irrelevance of the course she had been placed on. Despite many years of pastoral experience and leadership, she had been required by the theological college staff to study for a degree in Theology. Her expectations had been that the course would be more practically focused and, following several requests to change to an alternative practical course, she had now decided to cease attending her university-based lectures in the hope that this might induce some positive action in her favour. After a coffee break from a Thursday afternoon pastoral care session, the following occurred:

> After all of the students had left the common room, Donald and Fr. Robert came and sat on either side of me on the sofa. 'Has Lucinda been interviewed by you yet?', Donald asked. 'Yes, last week. Thursday evening I think it was', I replied, guessing what I was about to be asked. 'I know you can't tell us, but what did she say about why she is refusing to attend lectures at the moment?', Fr. Robert asked in a whisper.
> Research Diary extract

This request for information discussed within a confidential context, confronted me with the tensions arising from attempting to manufacture good working, respectful and ethical relationships with all participants in a setting characterised by the play of power between subordinates and their superordinates. Whilst on this occasion I did not infringe the ethical guidelines on assuring confidentiality (I informed Donald and Robert that I really could not discuss the content of Lucinda's interview), I had risked alienating two key and powerful sponsors:

> Donald and Fr. Robert did not seem pleased with my response. I wonder if there was any other way that I could have dealt with this? Could I have summarized or generalized Lucinda's concerns? After all, that might have helped her case. But what would the response from the other students have been if it had got out that I had given out information discussed in an interview?
> Research Diary extract

It can be argued, therefore, that there is a disjunction between 'the ideal' of formalised codes of conduct and the messy and complex field situations where some accommodation might be required (Grills, 1998:165).

My research project was focused on the occupational socialisation of these candidates for ordained ministry. The literature and empirical material in this area had foreshadowed the common experience across diverse professions that students' initial expectations of training are incorrect. Trainees experience the 'reality shock' of having to assimilate, adjust to and often contest institutionally approved versions of professional knowledge and practice, and that the realities of life in a training setting (especially a 'bounded', residentially-based one such as St. David's) are not just different, but generally the opposite of what was expected (Kleinman, 1984; Parry, 1988; Salisbury, 1994). In their work on the professional preparation and training of medical students, Becker and Geer (1958) had termed this 'rite of passage' the 'fate of idealism'. In common, then, with one aspect of what I was researching, I was experiencing my own 'loss of innocence' as my initial and idealistic notions of the professional practice of the ethical social scientist were modified in favour of more pragmatic approaches to surviving the field research.

Elision and reciprocity: how informed is informed?

Whilst I was generally open about the aims of the research, there was a degree of elision in that I deliberately sought to put the emphases on my interests in researching this occupational curriculum and the setting as a professional, post-compulsory education and training environment, rather than on the more sociological, 'social processes' of becoming an ordained minister that were also to be 'in the gaze'. Hence, I would 'talk up' my credentials as an educational professional and the bi-location involved in teaching 'A' Levels in a college of further education and working as a tutor on a teacher training course at a local university. When I talked about the research aims, therefore, I was always conscious to foreground my less threatening intentions to 'map the curriculum ' and 'describe the training process'. In truth, I was fearful that the label 'sociologist' would discourage disclosure and any hope of developing rapport. This anxiety was not alleviated by one of the students pointing out that 'sociologists, it is well known, are humourless, left-wing purveyors of nonsense or truisms' (Barley, 1983:9). To some extent, then, as with all research of this nature, there were 'degrees of deceit' operating throughout the entire period of fieldwork.

I adopted an active membership role which, as Adler and Adler (1987: 53) indicate, is fluid and 'liminal' as one falls 'between the margins of categories, groups etc.' Hence, there were changes and shifts in status and stigma as my identities as researcher, university tutor and ex-ordained priest led to differentiated receptions, interactions and, on my part, disclosures about my occupational and personal biography and the research I was doing. Anticipating some of the problems and pitfalls of undertaking research in an interactionally fractious setting, Donald had asked me at the beginning of the field work period 'how will you manage to be all things to all men?' In response to this challenge I quickly learned that degrees of disclosure, elision and rapport are dependent upon the complex interplay of situational necessity and personal characteristics. For example, I did not disclose to any of the participants that, despite the fact that I had been a priest, I was now an atheist. Obviously, there were varying degrees of curiosity about why I had resigned from ministry and, depending on the person or group that I was talking to, I would selectively respond from a repertoire of reasons. With the 'low church', evangelical students, I would talk of my problems with ecclesiastical authority and Roman Catholic doctrine, whilst for the more theologically liberal staff and students I would freely discuss my views on the unacceptable position of Roman Catholicism on the ordination of women and priestly celibacy. All of these reasons were genuine catalysts to my own resignation from ministry, but since my previous occupational identity as 'one of them' and of having been through a similar training and having worked in familiar professional arenas established me as a non-threatening and credible presence, I did not want to stigmatise my identity with total openness about why I had left the priesthood.

Becker (1967:123) argued that it is impossible to do research that is 'uncontaminated by personal and political sympathies', and that it is inevitable that all researchers will take sides (for a full discussion of this, see the chapter by Sara Delamont in this volume). The key question then, is 'whose side are we on?'. Establishing rapport in this setting inevitably involved 'taking sides'. For example, the community was deeply divided over the issue of the ordination of women and a focus group requested and organised by some of the female trainees themselves began to describe the ways in which patriarchy and prejudice permeated their experiences of professional preparation. Whilst I did listen to, document and describe the views and experiences of those opposed to the ordination of women, my own pro-feminist ideals led me to powerfully empathise with these women. This degree of identification was visible to some when I attended a 'clandestine' communion service celebrated by a visiting female priest who was not permitted to lead this celebration for the whole community on the grounds that it might offend those theologically opposed to her identity. My approval was soon known not only to those students present at the service, but to most members of the community within a matter of days.

At other times, I seemed to take elaborate care over consent. Since the setting was so small, to some extent the 'panorama' of social life was there to be viewed. This could have led some of the students and staff to regard themselves as being a 'captive population' who had no rights and certainly had no opportunity to say 'no'. Consent, therefore, could not be achieved in all situations and at all times. As with Salisbury (1994:67) I, too, wonder about 'the unintended consequences of my presence and of the study'. However, whilst some of the trainees may have objected to me observing lectures or activities that they were collectively involved in, no pressure was applied in requesting interviews and some students did decline my requests. With those who did agree, the BSA (1993) ethical guidelines were outlined before commencing the interview and opportunities were offered to:

* object to me recording the whole interview;
* ask me to turn the recorder off at points in the interview and that these would be treated as 'off the record' remarks;
* say and identify things as being 'off the record' even whilst the tape was running; and
* decline to answer particular questions.

In all of these interactions there were 'trade offs', as friendship and other 'services' were genuinely and sincerely offered, but also given in the hope that information would be returned (see Table 1, below). In a sense, therefore, any exploitation was met with some reciprocity, albeit insufficient.

Table 10.1 'Trade offs': facilitative tasks and acts

For Staff	For Students
Friendship	Friendship
Confidante and 'confessor'	Confidante and 'confessor'
Offering suggestions for Worship	Loan and donation of theological books
Setting up teaching rooms	Help in preparing an oral presentation
Contributing to course evaluation	Singing in the choir Sharing domestic duties

Conclusion

Professional codes and accounts that describe ethical issues encountered in the field are useful in alerting the researcher to the potential pitfalls and problems of undertaking detailed ethnographic field research. Ultimately, however, as Punch (1986:73) has indicated 'every fieldworker should be his or her own moralist'. These guidelines, then, should be viewed as advocating a situationalist and not prescriptive approach. As May (1993:43) indicates, whilst a loose and flexible system of 'anything goes' ethics is unacceptable, a rigid and inflexible set of principles would only leave us as researchers with one undesirable consequence, namely that 'the only safe way to avoid violating principles of professional ethics is to refrain from doing social research altogether' (Bronfenbrenner, 1952:453). Whilst elements of the research I undertook may have, at times, departed from some 'ideal', the participants in this study were never intentionally harmed or subjected to any covert research strategy.

References

Adler, P.A. and Adler, P. (1987) *Membership Roles in Field Research*. London: Sage.

Atkinson, P. (1981) *The Clinical Experience*. Farnborough: Gower.

Barley, N. (1983) *The Innocent Anthropologist: Notes From a Mud Hut*. London: Penguin.

Becker, H. (1967) 'Whose side are we on?'. *Social Problems*, 14, 239-248.

Becker, H. and Geer, B. (1958) 'The Fate of Idealism in the Medical school'. *American Sociological Review*, 23, 50-56.

Bourdieu, P. (1990) *The Logic of Practice*. Cambridge: Polity Press.

BSA (British Sociological Association) (1993) *Statement of Ethical Practice*. Durham: BSA.

Bronfenbrenner, U. (1952) 'Principles of Professional Ethics: Correl Studies in Social Growth'. *American Psychologist*, 7 (8), 452-455.

Carvie, I.C. (1982) 'The problem of ethical integrity in participant observation'. In R. Burgess, (ed.) *Field Research: A Sourcebook and Field Manual*. London: Routledge, pp.68-76.

Cassell, J. and Jacobs, S.E. (1987) 'Introduction'. In J. Cassell and S. E. Jacobs (Eds.) *Handbook on Ethical Issues in Anthropology*. Washington: American Anthropological Association, pp.1-3.

Coffey, A.J. (1993) *Double Entry: The Professional and Organisational Socialization of Graduate Accountants.* Unpublished PhD Thesis. University of Wales, College of Cardiff.

Coser, L. (1974) *Greedy Institutions: Patterns of Undivided Commitment.* Riverside NJ: The Free Press.

Coxon, A. (1965) *A Sociological Study of the Social Recruitment, Selection and Professional Socialization of Anglican Ordinands.* Unpublished PhD Thesis, University of Leeds.

Curcione, N.R. (1971) 'Family influence on commitment to the priesthood: a study of altar boys'. *Sociological Analysis,* 34 (3), 265-280.

Davies, D. (1998) 'Rites of passage in training non-stipendiary ministers'. In J.M.M. Francis and L.J. Francis (eds) *Tentmaking: Perspectives on Self-Supporting Ministry.* Leominster: Gracewing, pp.226-235.

Davies, R. (1988) *The Happy End Of Nursing : An Ethnographic Study Of Initial Encounters In A Midwifery School.* Unpublished MSc. Econ. Thesis. University of Wales, College of Cardiff.

Emerson, R.M. (1983) *Contemporary Field Research: A Collection of Readings.* Boston: Little Brown.

Emerson, R.M.; Fretz, R.I. and Shaw, L.L. (1995) *Writing Ethnographic Fieldnotes.* Chicago: Chicago University Press.

Epstein, D. and Johnson, R. (1997) *Schooling Sexualities.* Buckingham: Open University Press.

Fine, G.A. (1993) 'Ten lies of Ethnography: Moral Dilemmas of Field Research'. *Journal of Contemporary Ethnography* 22 (3), 267-294.

Goffman, E. (1961) *Asylums: Essays on the social situation of mental patients and other inmates.* London: Penguin.

Goffman, E. (1989) 'On Fieldwork'. *Journal of Contemporary Ethnography* 18, 123-32.

Grills, S. (1998) 'Ethics, Intervention, and Emotionality'. In S. Grills (Ed.) *Doing Ethnographic Research: Fieldwork Settings.* London: Sage, pp.163-165.

Hughes, E.C. and DeBaggis, A. (1973) 'Systems of Theological Education in the United States'. In E.C. Hughes; P. Thorno; A. DeBaggis; A. Gurin; D. Williams (eds) *Education for the Professions of Medicine, Law, Theology and Social Welfare.* California: McGraw Hill, pp.169-200.

Kleinman, S. (1984) *Equals before God: Seminarians as Humanistic Professionals.* Chicago: University of Chicago Press.

Klockars, C.B. (1979) 'Dirty hands and Deviant Subjects'. In C.B. Klockars and F.W. O'Connor (eds.) *Deviance and Decency*. California; Sage.

Mason, J. (1996) *Qualitative Researching*. London: Sage.

May, T. (1993) *Social Research: Issues, Methods and Processes*. Buckingham : Open University Press.

Measor, L. and Woods, P. (1991) 'Breakthroughs and Blockages'. In G. Walford, (Ed) *Doing Educational Research*. London: Routledge, pp.59-81.

Norris, C. (1993) 'Some Ethical considerations on Field-Work with the Police'. In D. Hobbs and T. May (Eds.) *Interpreting the Field*. Oxford: Clarendon Press, pp.122-144.

Parry, O. (1988) *The Journalism School: The Occupational Socialization of Graduate Journalists* Unpublished PhD Thesis. University of Wales, College of Cardiff.

Punch, M. (1986) *The Politics and Ethics of Fieldwork*. Beverly Hills. CA: Sage Publications.

Salisbury, J. (1994) *'Becoming Qualified': An Ethnography of a post experience teacher training course*. Unpublished PhD Thesis, University of Wales, Cardiff.

Smith, L. (1990) 'Ethics in qualitative field research: an individual perspective' in Eisner, E.; Peshkin, A. (Eds.) *Qualitative Inquiry in Education: The Continuing Debate* London: Teachers College Press, pp.258-276.

Van Maanen, J. (1988) *Tales of the Field: On Writing Ethnography* Chicago: University of Chicago Press.

11 Whose side are we on? Revisiting Becker's classic ethical question at the *fin de siecle*

SARA DELAMONT

In 1967 Howard Becker published his famous essay 'whose side are we on?' It is appropriate to revisit Becker's manifesto on values and methods, as we approach the end of the century in a swirl of controversy about postmodernism. The paper will scrutinise Becker's ideas and their utility for our era at the turn of the millennium.

The classic paper 'Whose side are we on?' by Howard Becker was published in *Social Problems* in 1967, and reprinted in his collected papers (*Sociological Work*) in 1970. Twenty-two years later Troyna and Carrington (1989) used the same title to reflect upon the research about 'race' and education in the UK, in a collection on *The Ethics of Educational Research* edited by Burgess (1989). Invited to participate in this volume, it seemed appropriate to re-examine Becker's question in the light of the swirling controversies around postmodernism (Stronach and Maclure, 1997) that characterise sociology today. The paper is mainly about qualitative methods, and more about gender than race or class. Becker's argument is explored, and the development of them by Troyna and Carrington, and then controversies around postmodernism are explained.

Becker's position

Becker started from the position that it is impossible to do research 'that is uncontaminated by personal and political sympathies' (p. 123), and that it is inevitable that all researchers will take sides. Therefore 'whose side are we on?' is the crucial question. He illustrated his argument with examples from the study of deviance, but all the points raised could have come out of his earlier work on education, in the Chicago public schools and the University of Kansas. Becker chose deviance because sociologists of

149

deviance are frequently told they are 'too sympathetic' to the deviants, and that this has distorted and biased the research. As he summarises the charge:

1) we fall into deep sympathy with the people we are studying
2) we believe they are more sinned against than sinning
3) we do not give a balanced picture
4) we neglect to ask those questions that would show that the deviant has done something pretty rotten
5) we produce a whitewash of the deviant
6) we produce a condemnation of respectable citizens (pp. 124-125).

Becker then examines the precise circumstances in which such charges are levelled at sociologists and concludes that the accusation of bias is levelled at investigations which give 'credence' to 'the perspective of the subordinate group in some hierarchical relationship' (p. 125). In deviance research the subordinate group are criminals, prisoners, deviants; the respectable are police, prison officers, judges, lawyers and the 'law abiding' citizen especially in the middle classes.

Becker then compares deviance research with educational studies, pointing out that

> professors and administrators, principles and teachers, are the superordinates, while students and pupils are the subordinates. (p. 125)

In all hierarchies, Becker points out, 'credibility and the right to be heard are differentially distributed through the ranks of the system' (p. 127). Researchers who refuse to abide by that 'hierarchy of credibility' are actually expressing 'disrespect for the entire established order' (p. 127). Accusations of bias arise when the researcher has not accepted the established hierarchy of credibility.

Given that 'we must always look at the matter from someone's point of view' (p. 131), and 'we can never avoid taking sides' (p. 132), Becker argues that the real question is whether our work is so distorted that it is useless. The central point of his paper is that good researchers have to strive to do projects which are not rendered useless by our biases. We must ensure that 'our unavoidable sympathies do not render our work invalid' (p. 132).

The Becker strategies for valid research are:

1) Do not misuse the techniques of our discipline
2) Use our theories impartially
3) Avoid sentimentality
4) Inspect our methods and theories to ensure they could disprove our beliefs
5) Make clear the limits of what we have studied (i.e. the vantage point adopted) (pp. 132-134).

Throughout this paper Becker had distinguished between research settings which were explicitly political, and those which were held to be not political, such as schools, hospitals and prisons. Accusations of bias were less frequently made, Becker claimed, when explicitly political settings are studied, because the disputed claims of the participants are overt, and have spokespeople in the setting.

Becker's argument became a classic, and, like many other taken-for-granted references, is cited more often than it is read. Soon after its publication, Becker's paper was attacked by Gouldner (1975) whose arguments form a starting point for Troyna and Carrington (1989) to whom I now turn.

Troyna and Carrington's position

Troyna and Carrington (1989) set out to establish principles upon which they could base 'anti racist' educational research, paying attention to ethical dilemmas and the tensions between anti racist theory and practice. They start not from Becker, but from Gouldner's (1975) critique of Becker, in which he argued that sociologists must strive for objectivity and give their ultimate commitment to fundamental values (p. 207). As they interpret Gouldner:

> this demands that the researcher's pre-eminent commitment should not be to black or white youth, teachers or administrators, but to the fundamental principles of social justice, equality and participatory democracy. (p. 208)

Troyna and Carrington then explore six dilemmas:

1) Whether white researchers can, and should, study non-white populations
2) Whether male researchers can, and should study females

3) Whether the 'fact' of Afro-Caribbean underachievement in British schools is actually based on decent research
4) Whether researchers have imposed racial stereotypes on their subjects
5) Whether any funding will be available for anti racist research
6) Whether research that exposes racism will get published by sponsoring bodies.

Troyna and Carrington looked to feminist activists in educational research for a way forward. They then propose that the collaborative, action research model of the Manchester-based Girls into Science and Technology (GIST) Project (Whyte, 1985) and the Girls and Occupational Choice project (Chisholm and Holland, 1986) could be a way forward for anti-racist educational research. In these two action research programmes, an innovation designed to change the behaviour, attitudes, and aspirations of school girls was established and was studied as it took place. In these projects, however, the school girls and their teachers were not partners in the research : data were collected *on* them, but they were not involved in the collection, analysis or interpretation of these data. They did not own the knowledge collected.

Troyna and Carrington felt that these action research projects did not go far enough to break down the barriers between researchers and researched. So they looked to Patti Lather (2001) a much more radical feminist than the two British teams. Troyna and Carrington's goal was to look for ways of developing 'transformative' research as espoused by Lather (1986), where the researcher works with the informants to produce 'emancipatory knowledge'. In such research investigator and respondents work together to analyse the data and develop theory.

Troyna and Carrington's invocation of Patti Lather leads us neatly to the dilemmas raised for us by postmodernism, and what Lincoln and Denzin (1994) call the 'fifth moment' of qualitative research. Lincoln and Denzin characterise this as:

> A messy moment, multiple voices, experimental texts, breaks, ruptures, crises of legitimisation and representation, self-critique, new moral discourses, and technologies. (1994, p.581)

If Lincoln and Denzin are right, and if Lather's attempts to remove the differences between investigator and subject are the best way to conduct research, many of Becker's ideas are rendered extremely problematic. In the next section the paper examines how current debates about qualitative methods and feminism force us to challenge Becker's analysis.

Qualitative research at the *fin de siecle*

The past decade saw a number of publications arguing that qualitative research is in turmoil: the quote from Lincoln and Denzin (1994) given above is a typical claim of this type. Because Denzin and Lincoln (1994) edited a best selling handbook on qualitative methods, their version of the past, present and future of qualitative methods has been widely circulated and has achieved an authoritative status. These authors divide the past of qualitative research into four phases, sketch in a fifth phase for the present, and predict a sixth.

Five phases are identified by Denzin and Lincoln in order to make sense of the development of qualitative and ethnographic research. Termed 'moments', each phase associates a chronological time period with a specific theoretical paradigm and/or paradigmatic challenge. The framework adopted by Denzin and Lincoln is well known. For the purposes of completeness I summarise it here. The five moments are identified as: (1) Traditional (1900-1950); (2) Modernist (1950-1970); (3) Blurred Genres (1970-1986); (4) Crisis of Representation; (5) The Post-modern challenge/the present. Denzin and Lincoln use their model to discuss the past, present and future of qualitative research across all the social sciences, and is clearly intended to be a broad characterisation of a considerable diversity of styles and disciplines. It is, however, all too easy for such mappings to become ossified, and they call for critical scrutiny in any evaluation of the current state of the art.

In the Denzin and Lincoln scheme, the time of traditional qualitative research (1900-1950) is the age of Malinowski and Evans-Pritchard in social anthropology, and of the classic Chicago urban studies (see Rock, 1979; Delamont, 1992). The first moment had an objectivist and positivist program, sustained by myths of the heroic lone fieldworker. They write of researchers in this moment: 'They were concerned with offering valid, reliable, and objective interpretations in their writings' (Denzin and Lincoln, 1994:7).

The second era - the modernist phase from 1950-1970 - in sociology is the heyday of the Second Chicago School (Fine, 1995): the period of Hughes, Geer, Becker, Strauss and Gusfield, when *Boys in White* (Becker et al., 1961), *Psychiatric Ideologies and Institutions* (Strauss et al., 1964) and *The Discovery of Grounded Theory* (Glaser and Strauss, 1967) were published. In social anthropology it was the era of Fortes, Leach and Gluckman, when anthropology came to terms with the end of colonial empires and focused instead on newly independent nations, Europe, and industrial societies. This second moment, a phase of 'creative ferment' (Denzin and Lincoln, 1994:8) is characterised as modernist, notable *inter alia* for attempts to formalise qualitative research methods. Becker's (1967) original formulation of the ethical dilemma: 'whose side are we on?' is a product of that era.

The third era, that of blurred genres, is located from 1970 to 1986. This sees the rise of many different theories, and the development of new data collection techniques especially tape recording and video recording. This is the period in social anthropology in the USA when Geertz (1973, 1983) and his influential concept - thick description - came to the fore. In British anthropology the structuralism of Douglas (1966, 1970) became fashionable, and challenged the older schools of thought. In American sociology the scholars inspired by the giants of the second Chicago school were publishing, and the Lofland textbook on qualitative methods (Lofland, 1971; Lofland and Lofland, 1984) appeared. In the UK qualitative research became especially influential in the sociology of health, illness and medicine (Atkinson, 1981; Dingwall, 1977; Strong, 1979). This period also saw the publication of the definitive UK textbooks on qualitative methods by Hammersley and Atkinson (1983) and Burgess (1984a). Publishers recognised that there was a market for collections of confessional tales by qualitative researchers. These included Messerschmidt (1981) and Burgess (1984b, 1985). The third moment is summarised as a golden age of the social sciences, with a main emphasis on new interpretative genres. There was a new multiplicity of theoretical orientations, paradigms, methods of data collection and analytic strategies.

In Britain, of course, it was not a golden age for social sciences and it was a particularly bleak time for sociology and education. The election of a Conservative government in 1979 with a hostile attitude to intellectual activity led to cuts in student numbers, reduction of funding, and a 'discourse of derision' (Ball, 1990) aimed at social science.

> Diverse ways of collecting and analysing empirical materials were also available, including qualitative interviewing (open-ended and quasi-structured) and observational, visual, personal experience, and documentary methods. Computers were entering the situation, to be fully developed in the next decade,

along with narrative, content, and semiotic methods of reading interviews and cultural texts. (Denzin and Lincoln, 1994:9)

From the mid 1980s Denzin and Lincoln identify a fourth moment - the crisis of representation. This moment articulated the consequences of the 'blurred genres' interpretation of the field. Signalled by the publication of Clifford and Marcus's (1986) *Writing Culture*, the ethnographic text was perceived as undergoing a crisis of confidence. Previously the text, typically the monograph, recorded the central processes of fieldwork and was the most important product of qualitative research. After Clifford and Marcus, qualitative research took what is variously called the linguistic turn, or the interpretative turn, or the rhetorical turn - with its accompanying legitimation crisis, described by Atkinson (1990, 1992). In the original Clifford and Marcus volume the authors became self-consciously reflexive about how anthropologists wrote up their findings for publication: that is, how the texts of the discipline were constructed. Recognising that all disciplines are, at one level, rhetorical, in that all arguments have to be framed to convince, or try to convince, the reader, the contributors to Clifford and Marcus began the task of reflecting critically upon the ways in which anthropology had been and was being written. Clifford and Marcus (1986) is now seen as the landmark volume, but there had been precursors such as Boon (1982), Edmondson (1984) and Fabian (1983). Since the Clifford and Marcus book there has been a steady growth of analyses of all aspects of sociological and anthropological texts from fieldnotes (Sanjek, 1990; Emerson, Fretz and Strauss, 1995) to publications (Atkinson, 1990, 1992, 1996; Atkinson and Coffey, 1995).

One of the consequences of the fourth moment is an enhanced awareness of ethnographic writing. In the Sanjek (1990) collection anthropologists reflected upon fieldnotes - how they are constructed, used and managed. We come to understand that fieldnotes are not a closed, completed, final text: rather they are indeterminate, subject to reading, rereading, coding, recording, interpreting, reinterpreting. The literary turn has encouraged (or insisted) on the revisiting, or reopening, of ethnographer's accounts and analyses of their fieldwork. Wolf (1992) for example, revisited her fieldnotes, her journal, and a short story she had written doing fieldwork in a Taiwanese village.

The fourth moment, with its reflexive analysis of textual conventions, coincides with the crisis of representation: 'The erosion of classic norms in anthropology (objectivism, complicity with colonialism, social life structured by fixed rituals and customs, ethnographies as monuments to a culture) was complete' (Denzin and Lincoln, 1994:10). The crises of this period put in hazard not only the products of the ethnographer's work, but the moral and intellectual authority of ethnographers themselves. The 'crisis' was not founded merely in ethnographers' growing self-consciousness concerning their own literary work and its conventional forms. More fundamentally, it grew out of the growing contestation of ethnographers' (especially mainstream Western ethnographers') implicit claims to a privileged and totalising gaze. It leads to increasingly urgent claims to legitimacy on the part of so-called 'indigenous' ethnographers, and for increasingly complex relationships between ethnographers' selves, the selves of 'others' and the texts they both engage in (cf. Reed-Danahay, 1997).

Troyna and Carrington's ruminations on how to conduct anti-racist research, and on the utility of following Patti Lather's programme stem from this period. The dual crises of representation and legitimation form the starting point for the fifth or present moment.

The 'fifth moment', the present, is characterised by continuing diversity and a series of tensions. Lincoln and Denzin write of this fifth moment:

> Qualitative research embraces two tensions at the same time. On the one hand, it is drawn to a broad, interpretative, post-modern, feminist, and critical sensibility. On the other hand, it can also be drawn to more narrowly defined positivist, post-positivist, humanistic, and naturalistic conceptions of human experience and its analysis. (Lincoln and Denzin, 1994 p.576)

The fifth era, that of postmodernism - began for Denzin and Lincoln (1994) in 1990, and is an era of post-everything. Patti Lather (1991) summarises postmodernism as follows:

> The essence of the postmodernism argument is that the dualisms which continue to dominate Western thought are inadequate for understanding a world of multiple causes and effects interacting in complex and non-linear ways, all of which are rooted in a limitless array of historical and cultural specificities. (p.21)

At its simplest, postmodernism is a challenge to the consensus held among the educated classes in the western capitalist nations since the Enlightenment at the end of the eighteenth century that universal, objective scientific truths can be reached by scientific methods. Postmodernism argues that there are no universal truths to be discovered, because all human investigators are grounded in human society and can only produce partial locally and historically specific insights. The impact of postmodernism on the humanities and social sciences has been considerable and traumatic. Because postmodernism denies that there are any universal truths, it also destroys the basis of any scholarly work which tries to produce generalised, universalistic theories of anything.

Stronach and Maclure (1997) explore some of the consequences of postmodernism for educational research but do not provide any comfort to those of us who wonder 'whose side are we on?' when postmodernism undermines the whole idea of sides. The journal *Qualitative Studies in Education* is packed with post-modern and textually innovative papers, but these rarely address the problem raised by Becker.

Ways forward

There are three ways forward for qualitative researchers. First, it is possible to reject the Lincoln and Denzin model, arguing that it is an inaccurate account of the past and present of qualitative methods. Second, one can reject postmodernism as many distinguished feminists have done. Thirdly, we can accept that education will never (again?) be non-political in Britain, and so educational research will never be non-political.

The Lincoln and Denzin model is superficially attractive. Many current scholars are attracted by the freedom offered by the diagnosis of postmodernity where there is:

> not one 'voice', but polyvocality; not one story, but many tales, dramas, pieces of fiction, fables, memories, histories, autobiographies, poems and other texts to inform our sense of lifeways, to extend our understandings of the Other, to provide us with the material for what Marcus and Fischer (1986) label 'cultural critique'. (Lincoln and Denzin, 1998:425)

However I am not convinced by Denzin and Lincoln's attempt to periodise the development of qualitative research, and even less convinced by the particular developmental narrative they seek to impose. It would be futile merely to criticise a framework such as theirs for simplifying things: simplification is inherent in such didactic and introductory texts, as Ludwik Fleck (1937/1979) pointed out many years ago. But their sequence of moments does gloss over the historical persistence of tension and differences. Each of the periods or 'moments' - especially the earlier ones -

is too neatly packaged. The contrast between previous positivist, modernist and self-confident (but narrow) perspectives, and the contemporary carnivalesque diversity of standpoints, methods and representations, is too sharply drawn. It could be taken to imply that all contemporary qualitative research takes place from a position of an intellectual field teeming with contested ideas and experimental texts (see also Atkinson, Delamont and Hammersley, 1988 for a critique of a different exercise in categorising ethnographic research).   Equally a chronological, and linear view of development does a disservice to earlier generations of ethnographers. Over the development of ethnography there has been a repeated dialectic between what might be thought of as a dominant orthodoxy, and other, centrifugal forces that have promoted difference and diversity. Rather than the temporal metaphor of 'moment' to describe the historical development of the ethnographic field, a more appropriate one might be that of 'vector', implying the directionality of forces in an intellectual field. This argument is set out in detail in Delamont, Coffey and Atkinson (2000) and more briefly in Atkinson, Coffey and Delamont (1999).

If we reject the linear model of Denzin and Lincoln, we can continue to follow Gouldner's 'objectivity', or Becker's careful self-scrutiny for bias, or adopt an emancipatory stance. We can resolve any conflict by ignoring any idea of moments.

A second strategy is to reject postmodernism. There are vocal and articulate feminists such as Joan Hoff (1994) the historian, and Somer Brodribb who see postmodernism as an attempt by white males to outflank the many non-white, non-male voices demanding a share of the academic cake. As Somer Brodribb (1992) puts it:

Postmodernism is the cultural capital of late patriarchy. (p.21)

Brodribb means that patriarchy in academic life is being sustained by a theoretical fashion which excludes all women, all ethnic minorities, all classes except the elite. Elite males have embraced postmodernism because it excludes all other groups, just as, Bourdieu (1988) argued the ruling class see as *inherently* superior cultural artefacts (such as opera and abstract painting) which actually owe their status to the elite's preference for them. Thus Brodribb uses Bourdieu's idea of cultural capital to explain the status of postmodernism among men. However, some women have embraced postmodernism, and Brodribb is savagely scornful of them.

She characterises these women, like Chris Weedon (1987) who wish to build feminism on postmodernism, as:

rag pickers on the rubbish heap of male ideas. (p.xxiii)

Brodribb is as hostile to postmodernism as Lather is enthusiastically in favour of it. If we follow Brodribb, we can also use Becker's guidelines in ethical matters, because rejecting postmodernism takes us back to the type of social research Becker undertook.

The trouble with this 'solution' is that it can make our research look reactionary and old-fashioned. The third possible strategy is to decide that educational research (since 1979) cannot ever be non-political in Becker's terms. Becker's political category puts the researcher 'in double jeopardy' (129). In political contexts there is not one single hierarchy of credibility, because the credibility is being contested by the different political 'sides'. Becker suggests that it is easier to avoid accusations of bias, because it is more obvious that there *are* sides with different stories. His example is the Los Angeles riots of the 1960s, but in contemporary Britain or the USA it is easy to see that education has moved into the same discursive space. Education is, today, a political arena. Ball's (1990) analysis of the New Right critique of education and their use of a 'discourse of derision', and the parallel analysis of the USA by Berliner and Biddle (1995) are ample proof of this. I have compared their analyses elsewhere (Delamont, 1999, 2000).

If we accept that educational research has become political then we can concentrate as Becker argued on 'technical safeguards' against bias, and follow his injunction to 'avoid sentimentality'. That means that we must not refuse to investigate things that 'should be regarded as problematic' because we do not want to know what is going on. So far so good.

However, when Becker wrote methods were seen as ethically contentious but otherwise inherently neutral. Becker, Gouldner and Cynthia Epstein all studied employment with different theoretical agendas, but regarded each other's methods as essentially 'the same' : technically different but politically neutral. Our problem today is that many of us no longer believe that. Instead we accept feminist methods, anti-racist methods, queer methods, and so on. Even if we reject the wilder shores of Denzin's fifth and sixth post-modern moments, we have abandoned the idea that there are value free technical methods which can be applied without sentimentality. Becker's dilemma is still with us, but his solution needs a rethink.

Acknowledgements

I gave a version of this paper to the BERA SIG on Social Justice in Warwick in June 1998, and received many helpful comments. Paul Atkinson, Martyn Hammersley and Robert Dingwall have all been revisiting Becker's paper in the late 1990s, and their thoughts have clarified mine. Karen Chivers has wordprocessed it several times with skill and speed.

References

Atkinson, P.A. (1981) *The Clinical Experience*. Aldershot: Gower.
Atkinson, P.A. (1990) *The Ethnographic Imagination*. London: Routledge.
Atkinson, P.A. (1992) *Understanding Ethnographic Texts*. London: Sage.
Atkinson, P.A. (1996) *Sociological Readings and Rereadings*. Aldershot: Avebury.
Atkinson, P.A. and Coffey, A. (1995) Realism and its Discontents in B. Adam and S. Allen (eds) *Theorizing Culture*. London: UCL Press.
Atkinson, P.A. and Silverman, D. (1997) Kundera's immortality. *Qualitative Inquiry* 3,3, 304-25.
Atkinson, P.A., Coffey, A.J. and Delamont, S. (1999) Ethnography: Post, Past and Present. *Journal of Contemporary Ethnography* 28, 5, 460-471.
Atkinson, P.A., Hammersley, M. and Delamont, S. (1988) Qualitative research traditions. *Review of Educational Research* 38, 2, 231-250.
Ball, S. (1990) *Politics and Policy making in Education*. London: Routledge.
Becker, H.S. et al. (1961) *Boys in White*. Chicago: Chicago University Press.
Becker, H.S. (1967) Whose side are we on? *Social Problems* 14, 239-48. Reprinted in H. Becker (ed) *Sociological Work* and in R.G. Burgess (ed) - see below.
Berliner, D. and Biddle, B. (1995) *The Manufactured Crisis?* New York: Longman.

Boon, J.A. (1982) *Other Tribes, Other Scribes*. Cambridge: Cambridge University Press.

Brodribb, S. (1992) *Nothing Matters*. Melbourne: Spinifex.

Burgess, R.G. (1984a) (ed) *The Research Process in Educational Settings*. London: Falmer.

Burgess, R.G. (1984b) (ed) *Field Methods in the Study of Education*. London: Falmer.

Burgess, R.G. (1985) *In the Field: An Introduction to Field Research*. London and New York: Routledge.

Burgess, R.G. (1989) (ed) *Ethics in Educational Research*. London: Falmer.

Burgess, R.G. (1995) (ed) *Howard Becker on Education*. Buckingham: Open University Press.

Chisholm, L. and Holland, J. (1986) *Girls and Occupational Choice*. London: Institute of Education.

Clifford, J. and Marcus, G. (1986) *Writing Culture*. Berkeley: University of California Press.

Delamont, S. (1992) Old fogies and intellectual women. *Women's History Review*, 1, 1, 39-61.

Delamont, S. (1999) Gender and the Discourse of Derision. *Research Papers in Education* 14, 1, 3-22.

Delamont, S. (2000) The Anomalous Beasts: Hooligans and the Sociology of Education. *Sociology*, 34, 1, 95-112.

Delamont, S., Coffey, A. and Atkinson, P.A. (2000) The Twilight Years. *Qualitative Studies in Education*, 13, 3, 1-16.

Denzin, N. and Lincoln, Y. (1994) (eds) *Handbook of Qualitative Research*. Thousand Oaks, CA: Sage.

Dingwall, R. (1977) *The Social Organisation of Health Visitor Training*. London: Croom Helm.

Douglas, M. (1966) *Purity and Danger*. London: Routledge and Kegan Paul.

Douglas, M. (1970) *Natural Symbols*, London: Barrie and Rockliffe.

Edmondson, R. (1984) *Rhetoric in Sociology*, London: Macmillan.

Emerson, R.M., Fretz, R.I. and Shaw, L.L. (1995) *Writing Ethnographic Fieldnotes*. Chicago: Chicago University Press.

Fabian, J. (1983) *Time and the Other*. New York: Columbia University Press.

Fine, G.A. (1995) *A Second Chicago School*. Chicago: Chicago University Press.

Fleck, L. (1937/1979) *The Genesis and Development of a Scientific Fact.* Chicago: Chicago University Press.

Geertz, C. (1973) *The Interpretation of Cultures.* New York: Basic Books.

Geertz, C. (1983) *Local Knowledge.* New York: Basic Books.

Glaser, B. and Strauss, A.L. (1967) *The Discovery of Grounded Theory.* Chicago: Aldine.

Gouldner, A. (1975) 'The Sociologist as Partisan'. In A. Gouldner (ed.) *For Sociology.* Harmondsworth: Penguin.

Hammersley, M. and Atkinson, P.A. (1983) *Ethnography.*   London: Methuan.

Hoff, J. (1994) Gender as a modern category of paralysis. *Women's History Review* 3, 2, 149-168.

Lather, P. (1986) Issues of validity in openly ideological research. *Interchange,* 17, 4, 63-84.

Lather, P. (1991) *Getting Smart.* London: Routledge.

Lather, P. (2001) Postmodernism and Ethnography. In P. Atkinson et al. (eds) *Handbook of Ethnography.* London: Sage.

Lofland, J. (1971) *Analysing Social Settings.* Belmont, CA: Wadsworth.

Lofland, J. and Lofland, L. (1984) *Analysing Social Settings.* Belmont, CA: Wadsworth.

Lincoln, Y. and Denzin, N. (1994) The fifth moment in N. Denzin and Y. Lincoln (eds) *The Handbook of Qualitative Research.* Thousand Oaks, CA: Sage.

Marcus, G. and Fisher, M. (1986) *Anthropology as Cultural Critique.* Chicago: Chicago University Press.

Messerschmidt, D. (ed.) (1981) *Anthropologists at Home in North America.* Cambridge: Cambridge University Press.

Reed-Danahay, D. (1997) *Auto/Ethnography.* Oxford: Berg.

Rock, P. (1979) *The Making of Symbolic Interactionism.*   New York: Macmillan.

Sanjek, R. (1990) (ed) *Fieldnotes.* Ithaca, NY: Cornell University Press.

Strauss, A.L. et al. (1964) *Psychiatric Ideologies and Institutions.* New York: Collier-Macmillan.

Stronach, I. and Maclure, M. (1997) *Educational Research Undone.* Buckingham: Open University Press.

Strong, P. (1979) *The Ceremonial Order of the Clinic.* Aldershot: Ashgate.

Troyna, B. and Carrington, B. (1989) in R.G. Burgess (ed) *The Ethics of Educational Research.* London: Falmer.

Weedon, C. (1987) *Feminist Practice and Poststructuralist Theory.* London: Basil Blackwell.

Whyte, J. (1985) *Girls into Science and Technology.* London: Routledge.

Wolf, M. (1992) *The Thrice Told Tale.* Berkeley, CA: California University Press.

Endword

TREVOR WELLAND AND LESLEY PUGSLEY

These chapters have illustrated and exemplified a range of ethical dimensions and dilemmas connected with qualitative research as 'reflexive practice' (Mason, 1996:164) and the active role that qualitative researchers and participants both share and play in constructing the research process. In this collection the contributors have explored a number of key issues and highlighted the significance of:

- informed consent and the inevitability of 'degrees of deceit';
- the management of multiple and sometimes fragmented identities and roles in the field; and
- reciprocity and the relational dynamics or personal detail of doing fieldwork and what to do with the information gained. This can include respect for privacy and confidentiality and commitment to more democratic and collaborative relations.

These issues and dilemmas are not unproblematic and, as the chapters in this book confirm, they play significant roles in shaping the research process.

Like earlier collections (e.g. Burgess, 1989) it is hoped that these chapters have encouraged and informed the reader in mapping their own ethical agendas for research practice. Along with the ethical statements of professional bodies, these chapters have sought to offer guidance and empirical frameworks within which informed practice can be adopted. They are intended to assist and scaffold reflection about the ethics of conducting research.

Silverman (2000) indicates that Weber (1946) has written of the scientific enterprise as a 'vocation'. For those who are actively engaged in research, whether at undergraduate, graduate or professional levels, our 'calling' is to understand something of the complexities of the social matrices and life worlds that we and others inhabit and construct. The experiences examined in this edited collection outline some of the ethical issues and dilemmas that confronted these authors as they responded to their calling. Whilst we cannot claim to offer any universal or proscriptive templates for responses to the many ethical issues elucidated, we have hopefully illustrated the situated nature of the choices we make in the field. Hence, whilst we can plan in the developmental stages of manufacturing research design, this can never fully prepare us for the messy reality of fieldwork and of 'getting in and getting close' to those who participate in our research.

In describing the dilemmas encountered in our own projects, we have sought to emphasise the fundamental importance of transparency and reflexivity in writing up the research, so that readers can appreciate the processes and interactions involved in data gathering and field relations, whether these be achieved via research diaries, fieldnotes and expanded accounts or analytic memos. These aids also serve to mediate a degree of 'communicability' (Rubin and Rubin, 1995:91), in that portraits of research arenas should feel real to readers. These reflexive accounts, therefore, have sought to nurture an awareness of the ethical dimensions and implications of undertaking qualitative research, and render transparent the often 'hidden' or 'backstage' elements of research process.

References

Burgess, R. (ed.) (1989) *The Ethics of Educational Research.* London: Falmer.

Mason, J. (1996) *Qualitative Researching.* London: Sage.

Rubin, H. and Rubin, I. (1995) *Qualitative Interviewing : The art of hearing data* London: Sage.

Silverman, D. (2000) *Doing Qualitative Research: A Practical Handbook.* London: Sage.

Weber, M. (1946) 'Science as a Vocation'. In H. Gerth and C.W. Mills (eds.) *From Max Weber.* New York: Oxford University Press.

Index